1965 WAR
THE INSIDE STORY

Defence Minister
Y.B. Chavan's Diary of
India-Pakistan War

R.D. Pradhan

ATLANTIC
PUBLISHERS & DISTRIBUTORS (P) LTD

ATLANTIC
PUBLISHERS & DISTRIBUTORS (P) LTD

7/22, Ansari Road, Darya Ganj, New Delhi
Tel.: +91-11-4077 5252, 2327 3880
E-mail: orders@atlanticbooks.com
Web: www.atlanticbooks.com

Published by Atlantic Publishers & Distributors (P) Ltd. 2025

Reprinted in 2007, 2013, 2016, 2017, 2020, 2025

Printed & bound in India by Atlantic Print Services

Dedicated to

Marshal of the IAF Arjan Singh, D.F.C.

About whom Y.B. Chavan wrote:

When Arjan Singh is asked to go ahead on
new task CAS walks as a dancing bird.
A real fighting Sikh. Yet how soft and gentle.
A jewel of a person.

Contents

PART - II: **UN & OTHER DIPLOMATIC INTERVENTIONS**

SECTION III

LIST OF ILLUSTRATIONS

LIST OF MAPS

Author's Note

What is this book about? And why at this time?

In essence, this book is an account of 22-day Indo-Pakistan War of 1965 as recorded by the Defence Minister of India in the form of day-to-day Diary in his own hand. It describes events, behaviour of key personalities, political as well as military, and their attitude during the military operations and diplomatic efforts to bring about the ceasefire. It also throws light on mental condition of those who directed the war operations. In that respect, the Diary is a unique contribution to history, more so, when one takes into account the fact that unfortunately Indian politicians rarely write memoirs, contrary to well-established tradition in Britain.

The War is an event that took place forty years ago. Since then some retired Army officials who were actively involved have written their memoirs. A number of books have been published on the subject. Most of these are about strategic and tactical deployment, actual conduct of warfare and decisions on operational matters. Present publication is mainly about the political and the higher direction of war, as revealed in the defence minister's Diary. That way, although not history, this book is a contribution to history related to that War.

Why the book at this time?

Some years back, I had published a book titled *Debacle to Revival—Y.B. Chavan as Defence Minister, 1962-65* (Orient Longman 1999). In that book, I had reproduced the Diary. As that book was a memoir containing political and other developments following the 1962 aggression by China across India's northern borders, the 1965 Indo-Pak War was dealt cursorily. Also, since the publication of the *Debacle to Revival*, several new accounts of the 1965 War have been published, the most important being of Lt. Gen. Harbaksh Singh's, *In the Line of Duty—A Soldier Remembers* and *Lest We Forget* by Amarinder Singh. Lt. Gen. Harbaksh Singh was the Western Area Army Commander and Captain Amarinder Singh (presently the Chief Minister of the Punjab) was his Staff Officer. Both have added considerable depth to the information available about the 1965 operations. However, they hardly touch upon political direction to War and diplomatic manoeuvring to bring about the ceasefire.

1965 War was unique in a number of ways. It was the first war that India and Pakistan fought after the partition. The seeds of that war were sown in the events following the creation of the two independent sovereign States. There was a certain degree of inevitability about the war. Despite another war in 1971, and the 1999 war that is described as the "Kargil Conflict", nothing seems to have changed. The same basic reasons underlying the war and the same modalities of Pakistan actively supporting and sponsoring, overt and covert guerrilla/ terrorist activities remain, as they did in 1965. In a way, India's leadership, out of their sense of restraint, fair play and endeavour to seek enduring peace and goodwill with the neighbour, seem to have missed opportunities to solve the problem. The Ceasefire Line (CFL), as laid down in 1947, more or less, continues as it was, although it is now called the Line of Control (LOC).

Recently, interest in that War was revived when Gohar Ayub Khan, son of the former Pakistan President, Ayub Khan, claimed that they had bought a 'Secret Plan' to attack Pakistan in 1965 from an Indian Army Brigadier for only Rs. 20,000. There is much speculation as to who that Indian officer could have been and what plan was sold. It is learnt that an enquiry had been launched by the Minister of Defence. Following those press reports, there was renewed interest about events in the 1965 War. Shekhar Gupta, eminent Editor of *The Indian Express* in an article of June 4, 2005, under the title "1965 in 2005, National Interest", remarked: "Bigmouth Junior Ayub may have fired a dud Scud but he's got us revisiting that War of Mutual Incompetence".

That was enough to revive my own interest in those events because, for three years between 1962-65, as the Private Secretary to the Defence Minister, I considered myself privy to the decision-making, projects and plans, including efforts to seek international assistance to equip and build capabilities of the armed forces following the debacle and several super secrets.

I, therefore, decided to refresh my memory and to study more closely Y.B. Chavan's Diary, to guess, if not unearth, whether India's operational plans were compromised in any way. That rekindled my own interest into events that preceded the outbreak, the operations on the ground and the international efforts to bring about the cessation of the hostilities.

The author has yet another personal reason. In 1962, when Chavan became the defence minister, the Army occupied a pre-eminent position amongst the three services. The other two namely, the Air Force and the Navy, were relatively small and lacked sophisticated equipment, although a deal for the acquisition and manufacture of MIGs from the Soviet Union, had been worked out. In 1962 warfare, the IAF had whatsoever no role to play. It started receiving greater attention, after Pakistan received American military aid and on that country joining the Baghdad Pact. Pakistan was equipped with F-104 Star-fighters, F-86 Sabre jet fighters, and B-57 bombers.

At that time, numerically IAF had three times the strength of Pakistan Air Force, but that consisted of mostly outdated aircraft. India's requests to seek F-104s, the most advance fighter aircraft at that time, were rebuffed in very rude manner. During Chavan's visit to the Pentagon in May 1964, the US Defence Secrctary, Robert McNamara, told Chavan: "Mr Minister, your Air Force is like a museum. I wonder whether you are aware of the variety of aircraft in your Air Force? You are still operating with Hunters, Spitfires, Vampires, Liberators, Harvards—exotic names of World War II vintage. All these aircraft are only worthy of finding a place in a museum." He suggested that until India disbanded that fleet, it was no use acquiring any sophisticated aircraft.

What McNamara said was true, but nonetheless offensive. USA did not offer any aid, and India's Air Force was mostly the same "museum". With that background, it was an exhilarating moment when some of those 'junk' planes, such as the Mysteres, Vampires and Hunters performed brilliantly against Pakistan's sophisticated F-86s. In fact, indigenously built Gnat, a small beaver-like small fighter, brought down several F-86s.

In 1965 War the IAF was deployed for the first time in warfare. In May 1999 the entry of the Air Force into the Kargil combat represented a paradigm shift in the nature and prognosis of the conflict. That invited nation's attention to the role that a sophistically equipped Air Force should play for defence of India. The saga towards that progress began with the momentous decision taken by the defence minister in the late afternoon of September 1, 1965, to launch air attack against advancing tanks and artillery of the Pakistan forces.

Air Marshal Arjan Singh, the then Chief of Air Staff (CAS), without a moment's hesitation, carried out tasks with great élan; and kudos that the CAS got from the defence minister, is recorded in the Diary and deserves to be widely known. That is yet another reason for bringing out this book and dedicating it to the Marshal of the Indian Air Force, Arjan Singh.

R.D. PRADHAN

Preface

The diary of the 1965 Indo-Pak War recorded by the Defence Minister in his own hand was found in Y.B. Chavan's papers deposited according to his 'Will' in the Venutai Chavan Smarak Library in Karad, Satara district of Maharashtra. Late Shri Shyamrao Pawar, a Trustee, made it available to me for publication in a suitable manner. I had reproduced it in my book *Debacle to Revival, Y.B. Chavan as Defence Minister 1962-65*, published by the Orient Longman (1999).

This publication is *not* an account of 1965 India-Pakistan War. The author, while familiar with the working of the Defence Ministry, the Army headquarters and defence formations, does not claim any expertise to deal with complex military operations. Deployment of troops and battles have therefore been dealt with somewhat sketchily, with the limited objective of annotating what the Defence Minister has written in the Diary in his own cryptic style.

During the last four decades, several books detailing the Military Operations have been published by defence officers of India and Pakistan. In describing the course of these events in the Indo-Pak War of 1965, the author has mainly relied on accounts given in *The Indo-Pakistan Conflict* by Russel Brines; *Behind the Scene* by Maj. Gen. Joginder Singh and *Missed Opportunities, Indo-Pak War 1965* by Maj. Gen. Lachhman Singh. The author has found material available in Capt. Amrinder Singh's *Lest We Forget* (1999) and Lt. Gen. Harbaksh Singh's *In the Line of Duty—A Soldier Remembers* (2000) of use in checking out material used from three publications mentioned earlier. Author gratefully acknowledges debt that he owes to all these authors.

This book is intended to highlight what is known as the 'Higher Direction of War' by the Defence Minister, who enjoyed trust and full backing of the Prime Minister late Lal Bahadur Shastri. For the author that alone is an important reason to publish the Diary. The Henderson-Brook Report of Inquiry into NEFA Reverses in 1962 India-China War had commented that the political leadership did not offer to the Service Chiefs sufficient guidance in shape of what is known in military parlance as 'Higher Directions of War'. Chavan had described that the main aim of the Inquiry was to learn lessons. 1965 War was a test, whether those lessons had been learnt, and how well? The Defence Minister's Diary may help military historians to make that assessment.

In order to help reader to follow the course of events, the book is divided broadly in three sections. The first section, Chapters 1–5, briefly describes situation on ground, Pakistan's intentions and India's military assessment. Second section contains the Diary of 22-day India-Pakistan War as recorded by Y.B. Chavan. It is presented in two parts. In Part I, Chapters 6–13, it has been reproduced in full, with commentary relating to the military operations and other matters referred to by the Defence Minister while Part II, Chapters 14–17, contains day-to-day extracts of the Diary relating to the United Nations and other diplomatic interventions. Third section, Chapters 18–22, is an overall assessment of the conduct of war, of relationship between the Defence Minister and the Chiefs, of lessons learnt after the India-China conflict in 1962 and Y.B. Chavan's reflections on futility of wars to resolve the basic issue that led to the first India-Pakistan war.

I hope that this publication may be of interest to students of military history, officers of armed forces and may be of use to political leaders, who are entrusted with the task of defence and security of India's borders and decisions relating to war and peace.

R.D. PRADHAN

Prologue

1965 Indo-Pakistan War had its origin in what Pakistan regarded as the Kashmir issue. In 1962, when China attacked from the northern borders, Pakistan saw an opportunity to create problems on the Western Front. Pakistan was firmly restrained by the United Kingdom and the United States. On the Chinese declaring unilateral ceasefire both offered military assistance to India. That had upset President Ayub, and Pakistan started strong propaganda against the massive arms aid to India.

India's position on Kashmir was made clear at the beginning of 1964 by the Indian representative in the UN Security Council. He stated that, "The threats of violence which have been emanated from Pakistan must cease." Then he added, "Once better atmosphere prevails, it would be possible—we are prepared to discuss with Pakistan all our outstanding differences." In December 1964, the Home Minister, Gulzarilal Nanda, declared in the Parliament political measures which would put the state of Jammu and Kashmir on par with the other Indian states under the Constitution. These measures included legal powers to enable Government of India to impose the President's Rule.

After this, President Ayub and Pakistan Government started preparations for armed conflict with India. Pakistan developed a four phase strategy to capture Kashmir valley by force. The first consisted of a 'probing encounter' in some place of Pakistan's choosing; the second, an all-out but disguised invasion of Kashmir. The third was a full-scale army assault by the Pakistan Army in the Chhamb Sector to cut off the Indian supply line to Jammu and Kashmir and finally, a massive lightning armoured attack to capture Amritsar and as much of other Indian territory as possible, to be exchanged eventually for Kashmir.

The first operation, code-named *The Operation Desert Hawk* was launched early in 1965 in the Rann of Kutch. On the outbreak of the conflict Harold Wilson initiated moves to secure ceasefire and eventually the matter was referred to arbitration. That set the stage for the second phase to launch a guerrilla type operation in Jammu and Kashmir, named Operation Gibraltar.

On failure of Operation Gibraltar, President Ayub Khan egged on by Zulfikar Bhutto, his Foreign Minister, decided on military option. On 29 August he sent a top secret order to his Army Chief General, Mohammed Musa:

> 1. ...to take such action as will defreeze Kashmir problem [sic], weaken India's resolve and bring her to the conference table without provoking a general war. However, the element of escalation is always present in such struggles. So, whilst confining our actions to the Kashmir area we must not be unmindful that India may, in desperation, involve us in a general war or violate Pakistani territory where we are weak. We must therefore be prepared for such contingency.
> 2. To expect quick results in this struggle, when India has much larger forces than us, would be unrealistic. Therefore our action should be such that can be sustained over a long period.
> 3. As a general rule, Hindu morale would not stand for more than a couple of hard blows delivered at the right time and the right place. Such opportunities should therefore be sought and exploited.

The operation was code-named: Operation Grand Slam.

SECTION I

A Momentous Decision 1

Place: Defence Minister's Office, Room No. 108, South Block, New Delhi. Date: September 1, 1965. Time: 4 p.m.

The Defence Minister was in a meeting with P.V.R. Rao, the Defence Secretary, Air Marshal Arjan Singh, the Chief of Air Staff (CAS), H.C. Sarin, Special Secretary, Ministry of Defence, Lt. Gen. Kumarmangalam, the Adjutant General and other officers. The meeting was to review battle situation in the Chhamb Sector, where Pakistan had launched a strong tank and armoured attack early that morning, taking the Indian Army and the intelligence agencies by surprise. The Chief of Army Staff, Gen. J.N. Chaudhuri, was on a visit to the Kashmir Valley. He had gone the previous day to review operations in Uri-Poonch area, where Indian troops had mounted successful assault to capture Hajipur and Kishan Ganga bulges in the Pak-occupied Kashmir (POK). He was on the way back.

At 4.30 p.m., Gen. J.N. Chaudhuri entered the defence minister's office and had a few words with Air Marshal Arjan Singh, the Chief of Air Staff (CAS). After hurried consultations for a few minutes, they sought permission for use of Air Force in the Chhamb Sector, where Indian forces were under pressure. He also sought thc defence minister's permission to issue a signal to attack by crossing the border.

Y.B. Chavan thought for a few minutes while everyone present awaited his decision with bated breath. In a soft and determined tone, he gave permission to launch air attack in Chhamb Sector and also to issue signal as requested by the

COAS for Indian troops to attack across the border. Defence Secretary, P.V.R. Rao, recorded his orders.

It was 4.45 p.m. That was the most decisive moment in India-Pakistan War of 1965. A quick and decisive decision by the defence minister saved India from facing a great disaster.

2 Backdrop to Operation Gibraltar

On the morning of 5 August 1965, at a village named Darra Kassi situated on south-west of Gulmarg, a young Gujar boy named Mohammed Din, while grazing his cattle, was approached by two armed men in green 'salwar kameez'. He was offered money for information on deployment of Indian troops. He gave them whatever story he could conjure up. As soon as two men left, the boy reported the incident to nearby police station at Tanmarg. An army patrol was at once dispatched to the area. In the ensuing clash, 7 intruders were killed.

It was learnt that there were several Pakistani columns sent to penetrate into the various valleys across the CFL. Similar incidents occurred near Rajouri. Three days later, on 8th August, two Pakistani officers were captured on similar patrol missions. Documents found on them and their interrogations revealed that these missions code-named Gibraltar would be carried out by a mixed force of Pakistani troops and Azad Kashmir battalions. The plan of infiltration was that these raiders would cross the CFL in small groups between 1st and 5th August and spread out in the forests on lower heights. These sub-groups would meet at selected points and then converge on the Valley from various directions. In Srinagar, raiders were expected to mingle with thousands congregating to celebrate the festivals of Pir Dastagir Sahib on 8 August. Next day, which coincided with the anniversary of the arrest of Sheikh Abdullah for the first time after the independence, marching with the crowds, the fully armed raiders were to capture radio station, air-field and other vital centres.

Meanwhile, columns further south and in the north-east of the Valley would cut off the roads to Srinagar-Jammu, and Srinagar-Kargil, to isolate Srinagar.

On 6th and 7th August, at several places, there were clashes between infiltrators and Indian patrols. There was intense activity across the border to prepare for offensive operations to cut the Indian lines of communication through Uri-Poonch bulge. This period also witnessed renewed launching of intense artillery bombardment on the CFL by the enemy. By swift action and re-deployment of troops, plans of the raiders for 9th August were frustrated.

19 and 25 Divisions (Divs.) had responsibility along the CFL, with 19 Div. looking after the northern Uri Sector and 25 Div. the southern Poonch Sector. In that sector, Haji Pir Pass was main access from POK and the infiltration route. It was located in what is geographically known as the Uri-Poonch bulge, situated on the main approach linking both sides of the Haji Pir bulge, and was thus essential to Pakistan for effective infiltration into the Valley from the west. From the Poonch side towards the north, a mountain range rose to dominant features named Raja and Rani and then descended to Betar nallah. An old road, dating before partition, ran from Poonch to Uri along the Betar nallah to Kahuta, keeping the Raja-Rani features on its right. From there, it climbed to the Haji Pir Pass before descending to Uri on the other side of the bulge.

On 1 August 1965, Gen. Chaudhuri, the Chief of Army Staff (COAS), had visited Srinagar to review the security of Kashmir and security of the CFL with the Western Army Commander and the GOC 15 Corps, Lt. Gen. Katoch. It was decided that the border posts along the CFL should be in the hands of J&K militia instead of the existing police and home-guard battalion. For that task, four additional battalions of J&K were to be raised. In the event, this decision had been made too late to have any impact on the emerging scene. By the middle of August, all formations along the CFL were engaged in aggressive patrolling. To relieve them from these duties on 14 August, a separate formation named Sri Force was formed under the command of Major General Umrao Singh, with its headquarters in Srinagar. It assumed responsibility for all counter-infiltration operations allowing 15 Corps under 19 Division to undertake operations along the border intensive patrolling that resulted in several skirmishes. On 23rd September, the defence minister informed the Lok Sabha:

> "As hon'ble members are aware, for the last 11 days we had been facing a new development posing a threat to the security of the State of Jammu and Kashmir. The threat has taken the shape of an organised incursion of armed personnel disguised as civilians from across the Ceasefire Line.
>
> In view of the surprise tactics adopted by the infiltrators and the type of weapons they carried, they were able to inflict some casualties...in addition 21 policemen killed, 5 officers and 41 other ranks (Ors) of the Indian army have died fighting the infiltrators. We have killed 2 officers and 151 other infiltrators and their bodies have been picked up. Another 300 are estimated to have been killed or wounded; 84 infiltrators, including 2 officers, have been captured so far."

In the light of these large-scale incursions, the defence minister was pressing on the COAS to take effective action to seal the passes that were used by the infiltrators. It had already been decided to capture the two bulges Haji Pir bulge and the Kishan Ganga bulge—the two main ingress routes to Srinagar Valley. That meant hitting across the CFL. The task was given to the 191 Brigade under command of 15 Corps. However, on the morning of 15 August, a major tragedy struck 191 Brigade area. Enemy fire hit the ammunition dump which blew up a part of the brigade headquarters. Brigade commander, B.F. Master, 3 Officers, 8 JCOs and 4 other ranks were killed. A large number were wounded.

In the wake of disaster, the COAS arrived in Jammu on 17 August and issued orders to proceed as planned with the operations. On 18 August the Army commander issued formal order for capture of Haji Pir Pass (at height of 8,542 feet). General Katoch tried to persuade to abandon the Haji Pir operations. Apparently, on the instructions of the defence minister, COAS again visited Jammu on 21 August to impress on the corps commander the *political* need for offensive action in his area of responsibility.

General Katoch, GOC of 15 Corps, who had earlier expressed reservations on the Haji Pir operation, again tried to persuade the chief to drop the operation. The COAS, however, made it abundantly clear that the operation had to be launched by 27th August. On 24 August, the Army Commander, Lt. Gen. Harbaksh Singh flew to HQ 25 Division to check arrangements for the attack towards Haji Pir from Poonch side. He learnt to his dismay that scope of the attack had been drastically reduced by 25 Division with the permission of the Corps Commander. Refusing to accept any explanation, the Army Commander ordered that the attack should be undertaken as planned. However, despite repeated assaults and large number of casualties, there was no success. It was on 26-27 August that the Second-in Command of 1 Parachute Regiment, a young officer, Major Ranjit Singh Dayal (later to become Lt. Gen.), led his column in heavy rains, over boulders and rain-swept nallahs and captured the Haji Pir Pass. He and his Brigade Commander Z.C. Bakshi, were awarded the Maha Vir Chakra.

The capture of the Haji Pir bulge was one of the most spectacular successes and the saga of those operations is by itself a glorious chapter of heroism and courage. Our troops had liberated the largest tract of territory in POK. Defence minister informed the Lok Sabha on 31 August of the success of that operation.

With the successful counter insurgency campaign and simultaneous offensive operations to seal off the Haji Pir bulge in the month of August 1965, it was expected that the Pakistanis would react forcefully at a point of their own choosing.

3 Geographical Features and Indian Army's Appreciation

The Ceasefire Line (CFL) in J&K is mountainous along with whole length except in the southernmost Chhamb Sector. It runs generally north-south in the Jammu province and runs west-east from its junction, west of the Chhamb along with the international boundary between J&K and Pakistan.

On the Indian side, the communications with J&K are tenuous. The nearest rail-head is at Pathankot and link to Srinagar by road was *over* the Banihal Pass in 1965, which remained snowbound during the winter. Pathankot, situated between the Ravi and the Beas rivers, with rail-head and an airfield, acted as a major administrative base with the military depots located around it. Pathankot-Jammu road runs parallel to the Pakistan border and is particularly vulnerable in Samba area. In any war, if Pakistan were to cut the Pathankot-Jammu road, or capture Jammu, Indian forces in J&K would face a logistical stranglehold, because they were dependent for a movement only on one road. From that angle, Akhnur bridge over the Chenab had been identified as the first target of any Pakistani military operation. The road linking Jammu to Chhamb, Naushahra, Rajouri and Poonch passed over this bridge which was unsuitable for medium tanks or heavy vehicles.

The shortest distance from Pakistan to Akhnur was via Chhamb. Pakistani forces were well placed to operate in the Chhamb-Akhnur area from their cantonments at Sialkot and Kharian. This was the only plain sector of J&K where Pakistan could employ tanks and heavy artillery in large numbers to gain swift results. On the other hand, for the Indian army

Chhamb was situated at an extremity of the Indian road system. Thus, while Pakistan could move troops in J&K from nearby cantonments quickly, due to longer haul from its cantonments to Pathankot, India could not. There were also limitations of the bridge at Akhnur on which heavy vehicles, artillery or armour could not be transported easily.

In the Valley, another area of strategic importance was Kargil. Kargil town was in Indian hands but the Pakistanis occupied high ground overlooking Kargil and the Srinagar-Leh road. During 1964, Pakistan planned of large-scale induction of guerillas into J&K over the spur. The spurt of CLF violation in early 1965 gave ominous signs of impending trouble. However, after the massive anti-infiltration operations carried out by the Indian Army in the month of August, Pakistan realized that infiltrators had not achieved much success. They had been forced out of the Srinagar city and Leh road.

Indian Army's appreciation of situation:

> Lt. General Harbaksh Singh, VrC, was General Officer Commander (GOC), Western Command, which included Ladakh, Jammu & Kashmir, Punjab, Rajasthan and Gujarat. The command was given three main tasks in the event of hostilities with Pakistan breaking out.
>
> 1. In J&K, plans were to be made to inflict maximum attrition of any Pakistani infiltration whilst also ensuring the security of communications within the State.
> 2. Insuring the security of the international border in the Punjab-Rajasthan theatre and destruction of any enemy forces penetrating that border.
> 3. Limited offensive operations would be mounted across the international border into Pakistan with a view to gaining territory, keeping open the lines of communication into J&K and destroying Pakistan's war machine to whatever extent possible, an aggressive battle of attrition.

The command included three corps formations. 15 Corps located in Srinagar had responsibility for the security of the

Valley, defence of Ladakh and to deal any advances by Pakistan across the Ceasefire Line (CFL) along the J&K border. Its tasks included to chase the guerrillas inside Indian territory and to attack their bases across the CFL. It was commanded by Lt. Gen. Katoch.

Indian Army Commander's assessment was that any major thrust by Pakistani Army would be in the Chhamb area. By cutting the line of control of the 25 Div. at Akhnur, the enemy would be able to isolate the Division and restore the balance in its sector. Accordingly, early on the morning of 31 August 1965, the Army Commander sent a signal to General Katoch, that he should consider holding a bridgehead covering Chhamb and the Mandiala crossing over the Manawar-Tawi bridge with at least two infantry battalions to check any thrust by the Pakistani regular troops. That afternoon, the COAS, along with Brigadier Narendra Singh, Director of Military Operations (DMO), flew to Srinagar to hold on-the-spot discussion with Commander of 15 Corps. Lt. Gen. Harbaksh Singh was to join the discussions next day.

Strangely, at the end of discussions on 31 August, the assessment was that instead of attacking in the Chhamb area, the enemy was likely to intensify infiltration campaign in the general area of Jhamdar-Naushahra. In consequence, 15 Corps task was re-defined. That was an incorrect appreciation and was apparently based on faulty intelligence.

The Attack

4

At 3:30 hours, on 1 September 1965, the entire Chhamb area came under massive artillery bombardment. Pakistan had launched operation Grand Slam. India's Army HQ was taken by surprise.

The area of attack by Pakistan regular forces in Chhamb Sector was cleverly selected, because it was a plain country wedged in rough mountainous terrain on the west and the river Chenab on the east. Pakistan could, therefore, use the armour and heavy artillery in this area, whereas because of UN restrictions and a weak bridge over the Chenab near Akhnur, India would be unable to induct easily heavy armour and artillery in the area. The nearest distance to the bridge was a vital bottleneck in our communications with Rajouri and Poonch. At the same time, from Akhnur, Pakistan could develop operations towards Jammu and block the only lifeline to the Srinagar Valley. Moreover, the area chosen by Pakistan lay at the junction of the Ceasefire Line (CFL) and the international border between the districts of Sialkot and Jammu. Thus, by crossing its armour, where the terrain was favourable, Pakistan could claim to have violated the CFL and not the international border. In that area, India could, under the Ceasefire Agreement, station there only limited forces. Pak plan was designed to exploit her armour and artillery superiority.

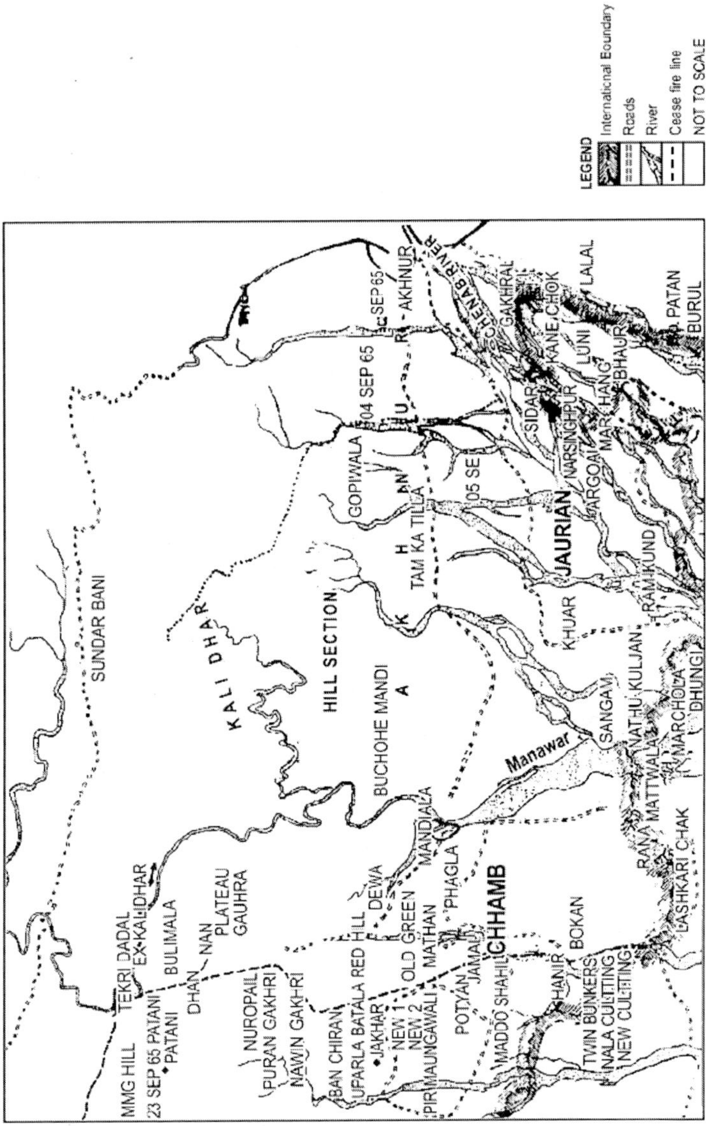

The Chhamb Sector

5

A Defence Minister's Diary

The Diary of 22-day India-Pak War, recorded by Y.B. Chavan, is presented in two parts. In Part I, it has been reproduced in full, with commentary relating to the military operations and other matters referred to by the defence minister. This has been done to facilitate the reader to follow the trend of events that are now over forty years old. Part II contains day-to-day extracts of the Diary relating to the United Nations and other diplomatic interventions.

A Page from Y.B. Chavan's Handwritten Diary

(6th September 1965)

SEP

6

MON

A historic day. Our troops marched in Lahore sector early morning. IAF also did a good day's work to begin with. We are not a war minded nation, and I cherish I am proud of it. Yet there comes a moment in the nation's life when it has to stand up against a bully and teach him a good lesson. That is what we are out ~~to~~ to do. We have no intention to conquer or destroy Pakistan. We are not thinking in terms of a ~~str~~ fight between a Hindu nation and a Muslim nation. We want a peaceful neighbour. And a neighbour who thinks he can get away with all his aggressive activities easily will never be peaceful. He needs to be told effectively in action that this will not do.

Well, my statement in Parliament was received with thunderous applause. After I sat down I found the Lok Sabha was different Lok Sabha — and I am sure India was new India.

E.C.C. met & took a review. In the evening things started moving fast. Pakistan Air force was hand with IAF. Did again attacks on Pathankot, Halwara, Adampur, Amritsar & Jamnagar. Took a substantial toll of our planes. CAS came at 11.30.

SECTION II

PART - I : **MILITARY OPERATIONS**

It should be noted that Chavan had recorded events either the same night or on the next day. Military operations have been described on the day these occurred, although referred to by Chavan the date on which he recorded his Diary.

Surprise: Pak Offensive 6

September 1, 1965

In the morning meeting, General Kumarmangalam said 16 days is the least (period) before Pak should retaliate.

At 11 a.m. visited the hospital. But the moment I reached hospital, P.V.R. Rao phoned to say that Pakistan, with armour support, had launched an attack in the Chhamb Sector.

Returned to office at 1 p.m. .... Fixed up further briefing in the OPS room, after COAS's return in the afternoon.

By 4.45 p.m. COAS & CAS had hurried consultation for few minutes and came to me for orders for use of Air Force in Chhamb Sector against tanks.

Had no time to consult ECC (Emergency Committee of the Cabinet) or prime minister. Time was vital factor. Took decision on their advice and asked them to go ahead.

COAS asked for signal to go ahead for Punjab action which I gave.

6.30 p.m. ECC, C.S. Jha (the Foreign Secretary), read out U Thant's report. Informed ECC of the air strike, informed the prime minister about the signal I gave to COAS for Punjab.

CAS came in the evening to report about strike and its results, "We are missing 4 Vampires".

In the absence of Gen. J.N. Chaudhuri, Lt. Gen. P. Kumarmangalam, the adjutant general, represented him at the defence minister's morning meeting. After India's unexpected and successful operations in the Haji Pir and Kishan Ganga bulges, Pakistani retaliation was anticipated. His assessment that sixteen days would be the minimum period before Pakistan launched an attack showed how faulty both military assessment and intelligence were.

General Chaudhuri returned to Delhi at 4.30 p.m. and drove straight to the defence minister's office, where a meeting was in progress. There he had hurried consultations with Air Marshal Arjan Singh, the Chief of Air Staff (CAS). The army and air chiefs jointly requested the defence minister to order the deployment of the Air Force against the onward onslaught of Pakistani tanks in the Chhamb Sector. The COAS also requested clearance to signal to the formations concerned to retaliate across the CFL.

Chavan approved the use of Air Force around 4.50 p.m. By 5.19 p.m., the first sortie of Vampires and Mysteres took off from Pathankot and gave a tough fight to the Pakistani F-96 Sabre jets. India lost four Vampires but that intervention gave some relief to the hard pressed troops on the ground, although some sorties in the ensuing melee hit Indian tanks and vehicles. Such losses were anticipated by the CAS. But the promptness of the decision and the quick action by the Indian Air Force saved the nation from a major catastrophe.

According to Chavan, he had no time to consult the ECC (Emergency Committee of the Cabinet) or the prime minister. He took the decision on the advice of the army and the air chiefs and 'asked them to go ahead' since time was vital factor. He also authorized issue in writing—in the form of signals—orders to the COAS to launch an attack across the CFL.

It was later in the evening that he informed the ECC of the air strike and got the prime minister's formal authorization to orders given to the COAS to launch an attack on the Punjab front.

As a footnote to history, it is interesting to recall that at that time there were reports that it was the prime minister who unhesitatingly gave orders to retaliate. Chavan's Diary throws light on what actually happened on the late afternoon of 1 September 1965, and his account is corroborated both by the then defence secretary and the chief of army staff.

The events leading to that momentous decision by the defence minister are also described by P.V.R. Rao, the defence secretary. He writes:*

> When the Pak attack came through, Gen. Chaudhuri was in Srinagar. He returned to Delhi at about 4.30 p.m. and came straight to the defence minister's room, where a meeting was in progress. As he walked in, the General asked for immediate air support, stating that he had just come from Pathankot and the air officer there was having the aircraft ready. Air Marshal Arjan Singh agreed without hesitation to go to army support, only pointing out that in attacks launched without adequate preparation, losses must be accepted and that pilots may make mistakes between friend and foe. The defence minister agreed that the attack may go in forthwith.

Gen. J.N. Chaudhuri's version as stated in his autobiography:**

> The day Pakistan moved her regular troops, infantry and armour, into the Jammu Sector, I was in Kashmir. As I was coming back in the plane to Delhi, the Director of Military Operations, who was in the aircraft with me, started writing out the required signals to go to the formations concerned. On landing, he went straight off to send them out and I immediately went to see the defence minister who formally confirmed my action. He then informed the prime minister, and that evening the PM asked me to see him, discussed a few details and further approved the action taken. He might then have informed some of his close colleagues, but this was not my concern.

During his lifetime, Chavan never contradicted reports that it was Lal Bahadur Shastri who had ordered the retaliation on 1 September 1965. By 1965 Chavan had come closer to Shastri and admired the prime minister for his low key but determined leadership in dealing with Pakistan's venture in the

---

* India's Defence Policy and Organization, *USI National Security Lectures*, pp. 16-17.

** *Gen. J.N. Chaudhuri—An Autobiography*, as narrated to B.K. Narayan, p. 192.

Rann of Kutch. Throughout the conflict and until Shastri's death in Tashkent, the two of them worked as a team.

India's Response—Military Operations

Facing sudden three-pronged attack by the Pakistani 12 Infantry Division, by the nightfall, the only brigade in the area, 191 Brigade, commanded by Brigadier Man Mohan Singh was in trouble. The Brigade operated under direct command of 15 Corps located in Udhampur.

The surprise attack on Chhamb was designed by Pakistan to exploit her armour and artillery superiority. After heavy bombardment, Pakistani tank units starting rolling. Indian armour engaged them but against the onslaught, India lost considerable armour. By the afternoon, the situation had become desperate. When at around 5.30 p.m., Indian aircraft launched an attack from Pathankot the situation on the ground was very confused with tanks and units of both sides in close combat. The hurried air attack hit Indian tanks and vehicles indiscriminately, destroying a large number. Many vehicles carrying artillery and armour ammunition were also destroyed.

By the evening as darkness descended, the Pakistanis had driven a wedge between Mandalia and Chhamb and reached the west bank of the Tawi and some of their units crossed the Tawi during the night. The Indian units started reorganizing defences while falling back towards Akhnur.

India's Armed Forces and security of the Valley were facing grave threat from Pakistani surprise attack.

September 2, 1965

(1) *I got further details of air strike in the morning meeting. It has certainly escalated the matters. But at the same time stabilized the conflict—perhaps temporarily in the Chhamb Sector.*

(2) *Shri (G.L.) Sheth (Secretary, Defence Production) returned from Moscow after doing a good piece of work in negotiating agreements for naval equipment.*

(3) *Meeting of leaders of Opposition...made a report to them regarding latest development. They were in cooperative spirit.*

(4) *Made a statement in the Parliament (Lok Sabha) which was received well. I emphasized the escalating elements in the situation by describing it as a "militarily developing situation".*

(5) *ECC Meeting—U Thant's report to the Security Council Members as discussed.*

I insisted on military advantages being maintained. Those U.K. proposals look like a trap.

Prime minister appeared to be strong. I hope he maintains this attitude.

(6) *COAS came to unburden his mind—looked somewhat depressed.*

On 2 September, the Indians awaited a fresh onslaught but none came. This was surprising. Later it emerged that the Pakistani army had changed command. Maj. Gen. Akhtar Hussain Malik, who commanded the troops was asked to hand over to Maj. Gen. Agha Mohd. Yahya Khan. This gave the Indian troops some relief and time to reorganize and reinforce their battle positions. Pakistani troops did not resume their advance east of the Tawi, until the afternoon of 3 September.

Chavan's entry shows that according to him India's air-strike helped to stabilize the conflict. It also indicated that India was willing to escalate the conflict in case Pakistani troops persisted in their advance towards the Akhnur bridge.

The news of the attack and a message from the prime minister that the Pakistani attack would be met and that there was no cause for concern, dominated the newspaper on the morning of 2 September 1965. That morning, Chavan, in a statement, informed Parliament that "the massive intervention of armour by Pakistan has escalated the conflict rapidly. We have to take an overall view of defence. Our forces are confident to meet any situation."

By nightfall of 2 September, news that in the melee our Vampires had inflicted damage on the Indian armour, and of the Indian troops falling back towards Akhnur under the pressure of Pakistani armour had caused grave anxiety. Chavan had found General Chaudhuri *somewhat depressed.*

In the meantime, the government had received the U.N. Secretary-General's message. C.S. Jha, the Foreign Secretary, had read out the message to the Emergency Committee of the Cabinet (ECC) the previous evening. U Thant stated: "(there are) alarming reports indicating a steady escalation of the fighting in the air and on ground, involving regular army forces on both sides."

In his appeal to the leaders of the two warring nations the Secretary-General called for peace.

September 3, 1965

This day began with a gift from IAF—CAS came to my residence with a news that IAF, in the morning air battle, had shot down an F-86 of Pakistan in the Chhamb Sector....

COAS came in the evening. He was in good mood. He said he was sorry that he was somewhat depressed yesterday, I can understand this. He has to open his mind, pour it out somewhere. It is good he is doing with me.

ECC at 9 p.m. Conditional acceptance (of U Thant's) was the proposal from E.A. Ministry.

My line was any acceptance now is unreal. Would affect the morale both of the people and the army and air force.

Prime minister took a self-respecting line.

What Chavan described as a *gift from IAF* was the outcome of a pitched air battle over the Chhamb area, India's indigenously built Gnat air fighters had chased and shot down a Pakistani (US-built) F-86 Sabre jet. That electrified the nation and raised tremendously the morale of the Air Force.

On that day the defence minister, along with his army and air force chiefs, had a long meeting with the prime minister to define the country's war objectives as follows:

(1) To defend against Pakistan's attempts to grab Kashmir by force and to make it abundantly clear that Pakistan would never be allowed to wrest Kashmir from India.

(2) To destroy the offensive power of Pakistan's armed forces.

(3) To occupy only the minimum Pakistani territory necessary to achieve these purposes which would be vacated after the satisfactory conclusion of the war.

These directions constituted what is called the 'Higher Direction of War' and would enable the army and the air force to plan their offensive operations within the framework of the government's aims and objectives.

Diplomatic pressures were already building up. The external affairs ministry was preparing responses to the message from the Secretary-General of the UN. While diplomats were at work, Chavan's mind was on the situation on the battle-ground. That is where his performance as defence minister was at test. Reports were not encouraging. On day 1, Pakistani troops had carried out a wide outflanking movement and taken Chhamb from the east, when the Indians were probably expecting a northward thrust towards Chhamb. The enemy had managed to occupy an area of approximately thirty square miles extending five miles east of the CFL up to the Manawar-Tawi river and six miles north of the international border up to the Chhamb village area.

After the lull in fighting on 2 September, it was obvious that Pakistan would launch an attack on Jaurian, situated on the west of the Chenab. The area is constricted between the foothills and the configurations of the Chenab. The ridge provided a good defensive position, blocking and dominating the two main approaches from Chhamb to Akhnur.

Military Operations

As anticipated, on 3 September, Pakistani tanks began to advance into the plains, east of the Tawi from where the Indian armour had already been withdrawn towards the right bank of the Chenab.

The Pakistani artillery scored hits on two gun positions which were damaged and the gun-ammunition started exploding. In the resulting confusion, the Indian gunners abandoned their guns. Pakistan pushed the attack and the local Indian commanders thought of withdrawing to Jaurian during the night.

Harbaksh Singh learnt on the night of 3 September that Lt. Gen. Katoch, commanding 15 Corps, had directly sought the permission of COAS to withdraw 41 Mountain Brigade engaged at the time with the Pakistanis, in the Jaurian area. Harbaksh Singh refused the permission till he had reviewed the operations at Akhnur.

September 4, 1965

(1) *ECC met twice 1 p.m. and 4.45 p.m. Reply to U Thant was finalized. Prime minister supported by most of us except Swaran Singh, who had taken unreasonably strong line.*

(2) *There were two air strikes. The afternoon one produced results. 2 Pak aircraft shot down.*

(3) *In Chhamb fighting, things are not going well. I think somebody has initially blundered. Jaurian will have to be given up to-day. Real fight near Akhnur bridge will have to be resolutely fought, otherwise it is going to be disaster for the army and the government. All efforts will have to be made to avert it. I propose to concentrate tomorrow on this.*

(4) *COAS came at 8.10 p.m. Gave me the resume of the events in Chhamb last night and today. He was rather depressed. Discussed with him plans of the next move fixed for tomorrow.*

I think that is the step that will change the complexion of the entire situation. If we fail there—and I cannot even imagine of it—the nation fails.

Military Operations

41 Brigade was commanded by Brigadier M.G. Rajwade. He reported that the Pakistanis were making preparation for

an attack on his forward companies and since he was not confident of withstanding the attack, he would like to withdraw. He was ordered by Harbaksh Singh to be ready for a counter-attack, should the Pakistani attack succeed in overcoming his forward defences. Both the attack and the counter-attack happened, and by 12 noon, fortunately the situation remained stable.

In the meanwhile, Harbaksh Singh learnt that the personnel of the 161 Artillery Regiment, deployed in forward position, had deserted *en masse*, leaving their guns, ammunition and vehicles behind. This formation came under the Divisional Commander, Maj. General Chopra. General Harbaksh Singh met him and the Corps Commander Lt. Gen. Katoch at Jammu airfield. He ordered Maj. General Chopra to muster as much manpower as he could and arrange to collect the guns, the ammunition and the vehicles. Only after having done so, he could then order 41 Mountain Brigade to withdraw that night.

Next morning, 5 September, he was informed that the 41 Brigade had come back safely, with all its equipment and ammunition. However, when Harbaksh Singh learnt that the guns were left behind, he became furious. He immediately ordered the corps commander to hold Court of Inquiry for this lapse. As a result of this enquiry, Maj. Gen. Chopra was sacked from his command.

Pak forces under the new command of Maj. Gen. (later Field Marshal) Mohd. Yahya Khan made a determined attack on Jaurian from the north, deploying one regiment of armour and two infantry battalions supported by field medium and heavy artillery. They overran India's forward positions. Meanwhile, a more serious threat was developing at Fatewal Ridge. Most of the defending units fought valiantly against heavy odds. However, there was one notable disgraceful exception, when the 161 Field Artillery Regiment abandoned their guns and fled the field.

Chavan's mind was focused on the *next move* and the consequences of its failure. General Chaudhuri was in a depressed mood because of reverses on the battlefront.

Pakistan's successful operations strengthened its determination to make a final push to capture Akhnur. General Musa, the Pakistan C-in-C, sent a message to Maj. Gen. Yahya Khan that day, "You have got your teeth into him. Bite deeper and deeper till he is destroyed. And destroy him you will, Inshallah (God willing)."

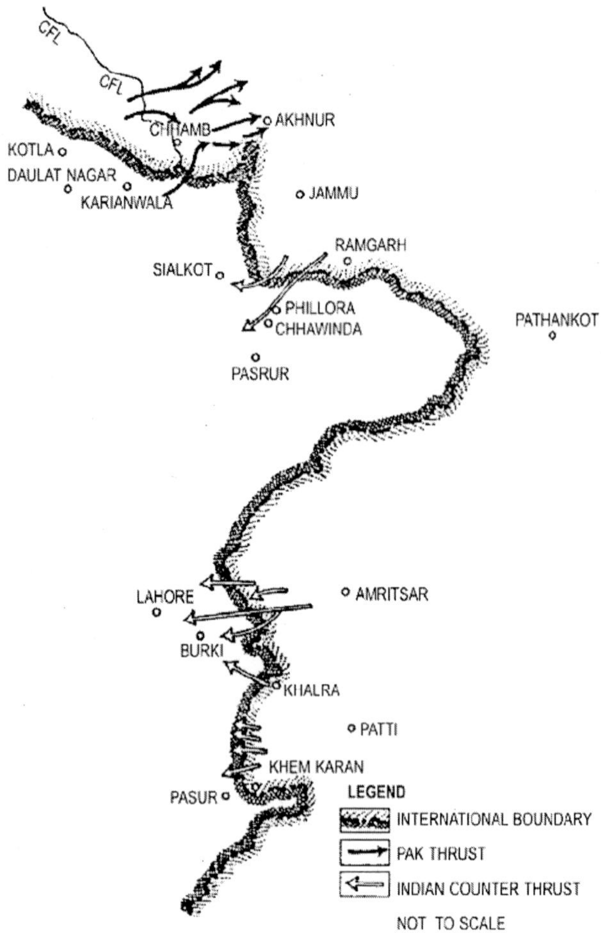

Pakistani Thrust and India's Counter-thrust (Western Sector)

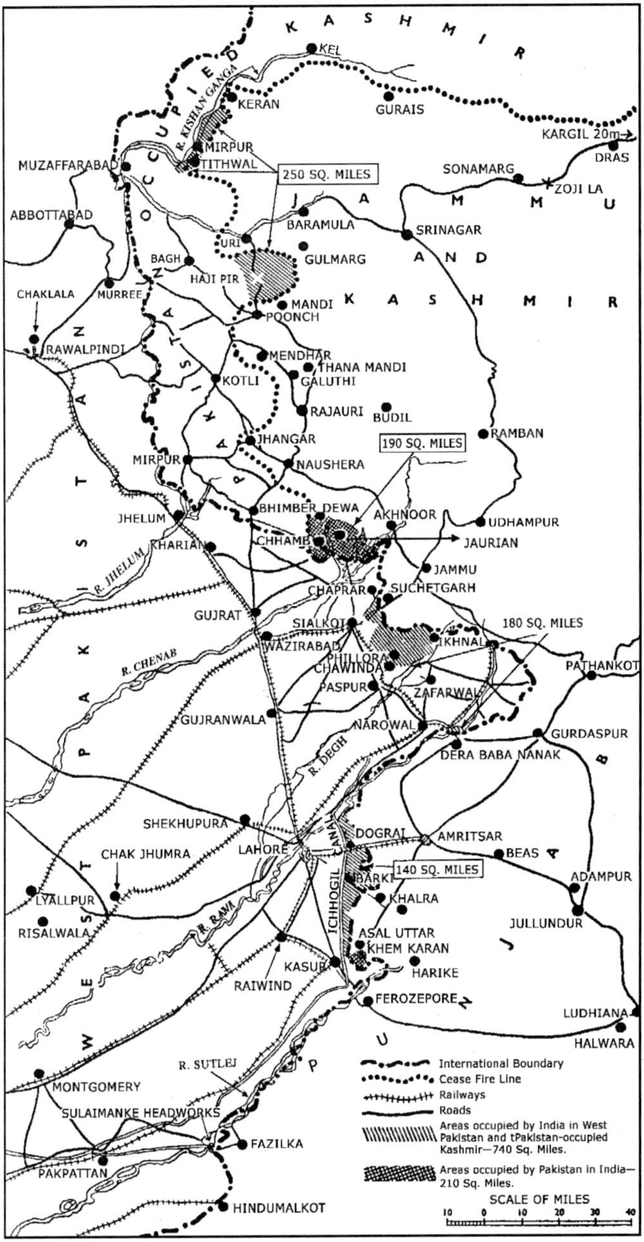

The Western Front

Operation Riddle: Counter Offensive

7

The situation was getting desperate. The loss of Akhnur would be major disaster. Chavan, with approval of the PM, directed COAS to go ahead with an operation that had been planned after the Rann of Kutch incident.

On 20 April 1965, Lal Bahadur Shastri had declared in the Parliament, "If Pakistan continues to disregard reason and persists in its aggressive activities, our army will defend the country and decide its own strategy and employment of its manpower and equipment in the manner it deems best." Following that clear direction, General Chaudhuri had worked out a plan, code-named Operation Riddle, for launching offensive action in the Punjab, taking into account importance of the area across India's international border with Pakistan, that included two major cities, Lahore and Amritsar in the Bari Doab. From strategic angle, the Bari Doab area situated between the Sutlej in the south, the Ravi in the north and the Beas in the west includes the most important areas and communication centers of either side of the boundary. Apart from the prestigious towns of Lahore and Amritsar it includes Kasur and Multan; also the Dera Baba Nanak (DBN) rail-cum-road bridge over the Ravi and the rail-cum-road bridges over the Beas to Hussainwala. Lahore is 30 kilometres from the international border, and Amritsar about 25 kilometres from the border.

Lahore, the second biggest city in Pakistan and the capital of the erstwhile United Punjab, has a historical pre-eminence unmatched by any other city in Pakistan. It is the hub of road and rail communications in the Punjab Sector in Pakistan and has a prestigious place in India's history. Its location near the rail, road bridge over the Chenab gave it an additional military importance.

Operation Riddle took into account geography of the area. In the event of conflict, geographically Pakistan had a number of strategic disadvantages vis-à-vis India, as Pakistan lacks strategic depth in the west and thus no vital area was out of reach of the IAF. At the same time she had tactical advantage as her cantonments were located close to the border.

Pakistan had constructed the Ichhogil canal a few kilometers inside the territory in Lahore Sector, linking the Ravi with the Sutlej parallel to India-Pakistan border. Similarly, she had connected the Chenab with the Ravi with Mararla-Ravi Link Canal (MRLC). The important towns of Sialkot and Kasur, however, remained unprotected being on the other side of the MRLC.

The Ichhogil canal formed a major obstacle for any offensive by India. While Pakistanis could cross it in their own territory, Indian forces, intending an advance to Lahore, had to fight on Pakistani territory and to face strongly entrenched opposing forces to cross over it. Thus, by its very nature, it could form a formidable defence line for either side, if they could occupy the bank on their side.

Till the 1965, India's operational strategy had been defensive and reactive one. Consequently, the deployment of forces along the international border was in defensive mode. Likewise, Pakistan had taken a similar defensive position east of the Ichhogil canal and it was assessed that it would *not* fight a major defensive battle east of the canal.

As soon as the conflict flared up, General Chaudhuri and the Directorate of Military Operations gave final touches to Operation Riddle planned as an offensive action to secure the eastern bank of the Ichhogil canal. It was felt that the mere presence of the Indian troops on the canal opposite Lahore would draw Pakistani forces from Sialkot and other areas and thus reduce its offensive capabilities in other sectors. Moreover, if India could establish a bridgehead over the canal, the

Pakistan army would be forced to fight there and that would lead to the attrition of her smaller army. By basing the defence line along the canal, India would confine the war to Pakistani territory in addition to acquiring a large chunk of Pakistani territory. Operation Riddle was planned to meet an eventuality like the one the Indians were facing on 4 September. That was the *next move* as noted by Chavan in his Diary.

The bold plan originally envisaged that I and XI Corps would launch simultaneous offensives in the Sialkot and Lahore Sectors respectively. While the XI Corps would establish a defence line along the Ichhogil canal, I Corps would establish itself along with the MRL. The success of Operation Riddle was based on a surprise attack on two sectors simultaneously. However, by 4th September the Indian troops in the Chhamb-Akhnur area had come under unbearable pressure and a diversionary attack had become desperately essential as Pakistani forces were poised to launch attack towards Akhnur.

After the reverses in the battle for Jaurian, the situation was getting desperate and the Indian commanders had to advance the attack by XI Corps for the night of 5/6 September. I Corps were still on the move to their concentration areas and Operation Riddle could not be launched as originally planned. Realising urgency, Chavan approved Chaudhuri's decision to launch the XI Corps into attack across the international border in the Punjab. That was a desperate move and carried high risks. Chavan recorded on 4 September that: *the step will change the complexion of the entire situation. "If we fail—and I cannot even imagine of it—the Nation fails".*

September 5, 1965

This was the President's (Dr. Radhakrishnan) birthday. Called on him in the morning.

Spent the morning in the office. Had detailed discussions with COAS and CAS about tonight's plans

At 11 a.m. prime minister called me to his residence where he was in conference with the chief ministers of all the states. I gave briefly the idea as to what was happening on the front in Chhamb.

N.D.C. met in the afternoon.

At 9 p.m. COAS came. He was relaxed. Had a brief discussion. I wished him "Good Luck".

On the evening of 4 September, there was mixed news from the battlefront. Little Gnat fighters had shot down two more F-86 Sabre jets of Pakistan. That was a cause for jubilation. But there was a cause for much anxiety because a Pakistani tank column had made a new thrust across the Manawar Tawi river in the Chhamb-Jaurian area.

That morning, Chavan called on the President Dr. S. Radhakrishnan to greet him on his birthday and briefed him about the situation. He then spent several hours with the prime minister to assess the discussions in the Security Council in New York and responded to the Council's appeal for a ceasefire. He also briefed the chief ministers attending the National Development Council (NDC) in general terms about the gravity of the situation.

On September 5, a single Pakistani F-86 Sabre jet had attacked anti-aircraft installations near Amritsar and inflicted severe damage. It was costrued as the opening of a new front in the Punjab and the same night the Indian troops launched a major attack across the international border towards Lahore, situated about 35 kilometers from the Indian border. Next morning, on 6 September, Chavan made a statement in the Lok Sabha. He stated:

> On the afternoon of 5th September, Pakistani aircraft intruded across the international boundary at Wagah near Amritsar and fired rockets at an air force unit. Anti-aircraft action drove them away. This violation was reported but there were further violations over the same border by the Pakistan Air Force and it was quite apparent that Pakistan's next move was to attack Punjab across the international border. The indication that this was going to happen was building up over some time. In order to forestall the openings of another front by Pakistan, our troops in the Punjab moved across the border in Lahore Sector for the protection of the Indian border.

> We have taken the decision to effectively repel Pakistani aggression in the full knowledge that the whole nation, irrespective of party alignments, is one with the government in this matter. The prime minister has received the fullest assurance from all quarters in this regard. I am sure hon'ble members and the country will show appreciation of the great gallantry with which our army has been fighting against odds in our State of Jammu and Kashmir, in extremely difficult terrain as in the Kargil and Haji Pir areas. The house is undoubtedly also proud of the performance of our boys in the air force who have destroyed several Pakistani Sabre jets. I have no doubt now that our armed forces will give a worthy account of themselves.

The atmosphere in the Lok Sabha was euphoric. Members lustily cheered the defence minister's announcement.

As recorded by Chavan, a decisive moment had arrived in the nation's history and for him, a moment that would make or break his political career. It was a historic day. He found that the Lok Sabha was a different Lok Sabha, and that India was a new India. Ironically, that day there was much public rejoicing in Pakistan as well. The news that Pakistani troops had captured Jaurian had enthused the people.

Military Operations

Midnight of the 5 September, Indian troops crossed the Punjab border. The essence of Indian offensive was initiative and surprising. The plan was to advance up to the Ichhogil canal and to capture the canal from Ranian, in the north, and Dograi on the GT Axis. The surprise of the Punjab front was complete.

XI Corps was commanded by Lt. Gen. J.S. Dhillon, a high profile officer. During night of 5/6 September, units of XI Corps started moving forward. 15 Division under command of Maj. General Niranjan Prasad was to secure the east bank of Ichhogil canal from Bhaini-Malikpur to Jallo bridge and to capture intact, the important bridges at Bhaini-Malikpur, Dograi and Jallo.

Accordingly, 3 Jat crossed the border north of the G.T. Road in Dial area about 3 km east of the canal. By 11.30 a.m., 3 Jat commanded by Lt. Col. Desmond Hyde were at crossing of G.T. Road-Ichhogil Canal. Hyde saw opportunity to cross the canal and his two companies crossed over with Hyde. This was a daring exploit of 3 Jat. This was the high tide of 15 Division advances as India's troops were not to cross the canal again because of confusion and cowardice shown by the 15 Divisional Commander and laxity by 1 Jat.

That night as planned they had captured bridge over Upper Bari Doab canal just across the border on the Pakistan side. The operational situation on the 15 Div. front was favourable to capture Dograi bridge on the Ichhogil canal. However, unfortunately, 1 Jat battalion that had secured in the morning the bridge over the canal in the Ranian Sector, became somewhat lax. They sent for their mess truck and started having their breakfast in the open when they were fired upon by the Pakistan Artillery. 1 Jat troops ran helter-skelter in panic. The General Officer Commanding, 15 Division on the GT Axis, thought that he had been attacked by two Divisions of the Pakistani army and sent a message to Lt. Gen. Harbaksh Singh to inform that his leading brigade had withdrawn to Gosal Dial, 7 miles behind the Ichhogil canal. He sought permission to withdraw behind the border. As a consequence of this hasty and panicky behaviour, it took two more attacks by different battalions and heavy casualties before the bridge over Ichhogil canal could be regained.

The situation was brought under control by the personal visit to the front by Lt. Gen. Harbaksh Singh, who ordered the brigade commander to move along the distributory shown on the map, and on reaching the Ichhogil canal, recapture the bridge on the G.T. Road near Dograi. Accordingly the troops moved in darkness. On the morning of 7 September, Major General Niranjan Prasad went in a Jonga to see the situation. This was to land the Indian army into a farcical situation that is described in the next chapter.

September 6, 1965

A historic day, our troops marched in Lahore Sector early morning. IAF also did a good day's work.

To begin with, we are not a war-minded nation and I am proud of it. Yet, there comes a moment in the nation's life when it has to stand up against a bully and teach him a good lesson. That is what we are out to do. We are not looking in terms of a fight between a Hindu nation and a Muslim nation. We want a peaceful neighbour.

A neighbour who thinks he can get away with all his aggressive activities easily will never be peaceful. He needs to be told effectively in action that this will not do.

Well, my statement in parliament was received with thunderous applause. After I sat down, I found that the Lok Sabha was a different Lok Sabha—and I was sure India was new India.

ECC met and took a review. In the evening, things started moving fast. Pakistan Air Force was mad with IAF. Did (carried out) angry attacks on Pathankot, Halwara, Adampur, Amritsar and Jamnagar. Took a substantial toll of our planes, CAS came at 11.30 p.m.

Military Operations

On 6 September, the Pakistan Air Force had carried out a raid on Pathankot and caught the Indian aircraft on the ground by surprise. Two MIG-21s, four Mysteres, two Gnats and one Packet were lost with no loss to Pakistan. There were raids on Adampur, Halwara and on the radar installations at Amritsar, Ferozepur and Porbandar. In addition, B-57s bombed Adampur, Halwara, Pathankot and Jamnagar during the night.

Pakistan also dropped commando paratroops on the Pathankot, Adampur and Halwara airfields. The plan to destroy Indian aircraft on the ground ended in a fiasco as the commandos were discovered and hounded out of sugar cane fields by the police and the villagers.

Of Cowardice and Panic 8

As described earlier on the Lahore front, the Indian forces had achieved a tactical surprise but the ground situation was not good. Utter confusion prevailed in the operations of the 15 Division under command of Maj. Gen. Niranjan Prasad. Three brigades under him were given the task of advancing astride the Grand Trunk (GT) Road and securing the east bank of the Ichhogil canal and started operations at 4 a.m. As described earlier, the 3 Jat astride the G.T. Road were stuck a few kilometres short of the Dograi bridge. Another column proceeded across the country towards Bhasin and the third one was given the task of capturing the bridge near the Assal Uttar. All the three brigades had lost their communication with division headquarters and their whereabouts were not known.

In the afternoon, when Maj. Gen. Niranjan Prasad went in search of them, he walked into an enemy position opposite Bhasin. He was fired upon and ran away. By the evening, the situation on the front was quite pathetic. The divisional commander had just managed to evade capture and the commanding officers of two battalions had lost their mental balance and were unfit to lead their units. On learning that, Lt. Gen. Harbaksh Singh and the corps commander drove in a Jonga to the battlefront. Army commander found that the enemy air-attack had created a havoc on G.T. Road. Vehicles were burning and several vehicles of 15 Division abandoned on the road, the drivers having run away, leaving some of the engines still running. Major General Niranjan Prasad was hiding in a recently irrigated sugar cane field. As described by Harbaksh Singh: 'He came out to receive us, with his boots covered with wet mud. He had no head cover, nor was he wearing any badges of rank. He had stubble on his face, not having shaved.' Seeing him in such a stage, Harbaksh Singh asked him: 'Whether he was the General Officer commanding a division or a coolie? Why had he removed badges of rank and not shaved? Niranjan Prasad had no answer. Lt. Gen. Harbaksh Singh ordered 15 Division to re-capture the bridge of the G.T. Road and the divisional commander was asked to report the progress of the operations to the corps commander next morning.

Major General Niranjan Prasad had generally a poor record in operational command. In NEFA during 1962 operations and later while commanding Infantry Division at Rajouri, he had been found deficient. Despite Harbaksh Singh requesting Gen. Chaudhuri to replace him, the chief disregarded the suggestion. Niranjan Prasad had a penchant for making representations. That morning, after being found in that embarrassing situation, he had apparently threatened representation against the higher-ups. He had kept one ready in his briefcase along with some secret and confidential papers.

Next morning, i.e. 7 September, Niranjan Prasad undertook visit to the front to see progress of operations of his brigade as directed previous day by Harbaksh Singh. He was in a Jonga with his ADC, with two jeeps following him as escort. As he progressed along the canal distributaries, he was fired at by a distant medium machine gun. Both he and his ADC abandoned the Jonga and took cover in a field of crops nearby, as did the escort. A little later, Niranjan Prasad decided to return to his headquarters in one of the escort jeeps. As he drove off, the second escort jeep followed him. In that confusion, the Jonga, with formation flag and star-plates, which he had driven to the front was left behind with his briefcase. Subsequently, this was captured by the Pakistanis, who used the Jonga for propaganda. They also started broadcasting the contents of his briefcase, including his representations against Lt. Gen. Harbaksh Singh.

On the basis of enquiry by GOC XI Corps, Niranjan Prasad was to face court martial but the COAS sent for Maj. Niranjan Prasad and asked him to resign.

September 7, 1965

I had not slept well last night. 9.45 a.m.—morning meeting—Army is doing well according to plans. CAS gave further bad news of losses at Kulaikunda and over a base in West Pakistan.

Bombing by both sides in East Pakistan has created a problem. I told CAS to hold his hand in East Pakistan. We do not want any wasteful escalation there. Politically also, it would be unwise to do anything which might provoke China at this moment. He (CAS) agreed.

ECC was concerned about air-raids on our bases. When ECC was on, information about good work of army in Chhamb Sector came. The news of Dera Baba Nanak bridge being exploded arrived. In the afternoon good news of IAF taking a good toll of 2 F-104's came. I must say I started feeling well.

Executive Members (Congress Parliament Party's) at 4 p.m. were interesting. They were quite appreciative. Parliamentary Board met at 6.30 (p.m.). I was somewhat late. Decided to postpone organizational elections. N.G. Gore came to see me at 8 p.m.

Chavan's reference to the Dera Baba Nanak bridge was in connection with the operation launched by 29 Infantry Brigade. It was given the task of eliminating the small Pakistani enclave and to capture the rail-cum-road bridge over the Ravi intact, if possible. On 6 September, the Indians concentrated their fire to destroy the tower where Pakistan had built strong defences, without success. During the battle some Pakistani troops crossed the bridge and attacked Indian positions. Next night when the Indian armour pushed them back, retreating Pakistani forces blew up one of the spans of the bridge.

Unexpectedly, difficult situation had arisen in the east, when the Pakistan Air Force attacked Kulaikunda in West

Bengal. They also dropped some paratroops between Guwahati and Shillong in Assam. All of them were captured.

Chavan did not want any escalation in the east and had advised CAS not to initiate any action on that side. However, due to some misunderstanding, that day Canberras of the Eastern Air Command attacked Chittagong and Dacca airfields. In retaliation, the Pakistan Air Force attacked Indian bases at Kulaikunda, Bagdogra and Calcutta, hitting a number of aircraft on the ground.

Early that morning, the Indian Air Force had launched an offensive by attacking Sargodha, the most important Air Force station in Pakistan. There were four raids on Sargodha that day.

September 8, 1965

No entry in the Diary.

September 9, 1965

Had a very hard day on all the fronts. Very fierce counter-attacks mounted and we are required to withdraw in Kasur area.

COAS was somewhat uncertain of himself. I suggested to him that he should go in forward areas so that he will be in touch of (with) realities. He said he would go next day.

Chavan's reference to *very fierce counter-attacks* related to the great tank battle that was taking shape in the Khem Karan sector of the Punjab. Battle situation on the Khem Karan front was causing great deal of anxiety.

Military Operations

Khem Karan and Kasur are twin townships about 10 km apart, with the international boundary running halfway between the two. Rohi/Kasur nallah runs in a horse-shoe shape around Khem Karan in both Indian and Pakistani territory. Kasur nallah and the Ichhogil canal beyond that acted as obstacles to any advance by Indian troops to Kasur town.

XI Corps earmarked 4 Mountain Division under Maj. Gen. Gurbaksh Singh for operation in Khem Karan Sector. It had planned for 62 Brigade to establish a firm base south-west of Khem Karan, while the 7 Brigade was to clear the east bank of the Ichhogil canal simultaneously.

During the operation, leading Brigade of 4 Mountain Division, which had the Ichhogil canal as its objective, stopped short of it, mistaking a small nallah to be the canal. That afternoon after a heavy bombardment, Pak tanks suddenly emerged *from underneath* the Ichhogil canal. Indian army had no knowledge of the existence of these underground ducts. The sudden attack unnerved 13 Dogra battalion. Fearing onrush by tanks and heavy artillery fire the battalion abandoned its position. Throughout the night of 6/7 September they were attacked by an overwhelming force of armour (Pattons) and infantry. Under a collapsing command and control in the dark, units were disintegrating and 4 Mountain Division that included 6 Infantry Battalions had been reduced to about 3-1/2. This reduction was mostly due to desertion. Maj. Gen. Gurbaksh Singh, realising the gravity of the deteriorating situation of 62 Brigade, ordered 7 Brigade to fall back to Assal Uttar. The brigade commanders and regimental officers rose to the occasion to check the rot. Using threats, calls to honour and other means, small bodies of men who were strugglers were assembled and led to their unit defended areas.

The tactical situation on 7 September remained in a state of flux without much fighting. However, the overall situation remained worrisome. Of the 6 battalions under 4 Division only two had remained intact. The morale of the Division was low and it was recommended by Lt. Gen. Joginder Singh, the GOC XI Corps that 4 Mountain Division should be replaced and all its Infantry Units except the two be dismantled. This was very grave situation on the battlefront at a time when Pakistani tank formations were on the move. Fortunately, this great blunder resulting in panic and *irregular retreat* was matched by the Pakistani Command and their tank formation were to meet their Waterloo at Assal Uttar.

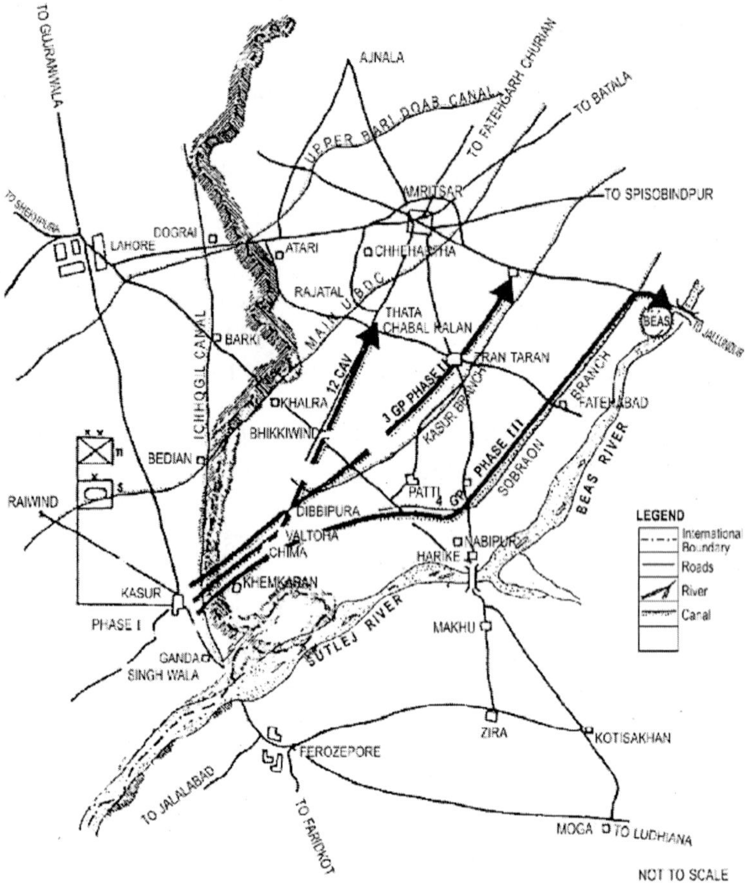

Pak Offensive Plan—Khemkaran Sector

Turning the Corner

9

Two great tank battles of the 1965 War were taking shape almost at the same time: one in Khem Karan Sector and the other in Sialkot Sector.

By the evening of 8 September, both India and Pakistan had shown their hand by committing their respective armoured divisions in Chhawinda in the Sialkot Sector and Khem Karan in Lahore Sector. The outcome of the war was hinged on the fate of the respective armoured offensives. In Khem Karan Sector, Pakistani commander's plan was to launch a frontal attack on 4 Division's defended area by cutting off the Khem Karan-Bhikkiwind road in Cheema area by a left hook.

At that stage of battle, as described earlier, on the Lahore front, although the Indian forces had achieved tactical surprise, the overall situation was not good. Utter confusion prevailed in the operations of the 15 Division and by the evening of 8 September, situation was indeed pathetic. The division commander had just managed to evade capture. The commanding officers of two battalions had lost mental balance and were unfit to lead their units. The Army Commander Lt. Gen. Harbaksh Singh had acted decisively and relieved the Divisional Commander Maj. Gen. Niranjan Prasad and the two CO's of their command. Next day a new division commander hurriedly inducted from the army HQ had taken over. New Commander, Maj. Gen. Mohinder Singh, found the situation chaotic and morale of the troops low.

Military Operations

The village of Assal Uttar lies in the fork of Khem Karan-Patti road and Khem Karan-Bhikkiwind and blocks both these approaches. The area is flat and cultivated with sugarcane. A number of water channels in the area could be cut to flood the area and restrict enemy armour mobility. Retreating Indian tank commanders laid a horse-shoe trap near Assal Uttar. The Indians had worked out a well thought-out deployment for dealing with the expected threat.

On 8 September, at 14:30 hours, Pakistan launched their first armoured attack in three columns. That afternoon during the first hour of the engagement, the Indian Centurions destroyed five Pattons and one Chaffe. The Pakistani column withdrew and made another attempt to break the Indian defences at Cheema. They were allowed to get into the horse-shoe and in the ensuring fierce counter-attack, several Pattons were destroyed.

On 9 September, Pak central column advanced over Bhikkiwind axis passing through Assal Uttar. They were stopped there by our dug-down tanks. Intense artillery fire was directed at Indian tank formation. However, because of tall crops and proximity of the opposing tanks it was difficult to pinpoint the fire. A number of Pak tanks were destroyed. Pakistan's armoured division equipped with Pattons could not make any dent in hastily prepared defences of debilitated 4 Divisions. India's three squadrons of 9 Horse stood against the might of 1 Pak Armoured Division. Our crew of the Shermans and Centurions had overcome the awe of the mighty Pattons.

On 10 September Pakistan's operations started early. About 8.30 a.m., Pak tanks approached astride Bhikkiwind road. Nine Horse tanks waited in their dug-down positions. When Pak tanks were within 100 meters, their four tanks were knocked down. Their infantry got separated. In the attack mounted in the afternoon a number of Pak tanks were destroyed. At this stage, as is now known from accounts of Pak generals, their GOC's directing the battle got desperate. They ordered their Armoured Brigade Commander to get up and go forward in the name of *Islam, Pakistan and Hilat-e-Jurat*. They launched a desperate attack. Havildar Hamid of 4 Grenadiers who was manning a jeep mounted RCL 9 (Recoil Less Guns), opened fire at point-blank range, destroying three

Pattons and disabling the fourth. Hamid was killed on the spot. For his bravery on battlefield Abdul Hamid was awarded posthumous Param Vir Chakra (PVC).

Throughout the night of 10/11 September, the Indian guns had bombarded and tank formations got ready for battle. They were surprised that there was no response to their fire from the Pakistani tanks. They found 25 enemy tanks, some with engines running and wireless sets on were abandoned in the waterlogged sugar cane fields. Major Suresh Vadera, Squadron of India's 3 Cavalry, captured 9 serviceable Pattons. He was later awarded Maha Vir Chara (MVC). Pakistan's final thrust met the same fate. The battle of Assal Uttar had been won. Lt. Col. Arun Kumar Vaidya of the Deccan Horse was also awarded MVC. Later in his career he rose to become the Chief of Army Staff.

The news of Pak defeat in Assal Uttar and news of the capture of squadron worth of abundant serviceable Pattons was received with electric effect. After the ceasefire, about 70 Pattons were collected near Bhikkiwind and the place was named Patton Nagar.

The tank battle at Assal Uttar was a decisive moment that tilted the balance in India's favour.

September 10, 1965

ECC was the usual affair, Indira Gandhi (the Information and Broadcasting Minister) took rather unhelpful attitude about publicity. As we are not in a position to give more material to them, they (her Ministry) are becoming somewhat unpopular with the Press and (therefore) we should take over the briefing. I thought it was selfish and said so.

Made a Statement in Lok Sabha (in the) evening mentioning withdrawal of Kasur.

COAS met in the evening briefing meeting. His visit to forward areas has done him quite good.

He was more certain (sure) of himself.

On 9 September, Chavan had found COAS uncertain of himself on receiving XI Corps Commander Lt. Gen. Joginder Singh's suggestion to immediately replace 4 Mountain Division while fierce fighting was taking place. Chavan suggested to

COAS to visit the front to make on the spot assessment. As described by Harbaksh Singh:

> Late at night on 9 September, the Chief of Army Staff rang me up to say that he had read Corps Commander XI Corps' letter sent to me and that his advice was to save the whole army from being cut off by Pakistan's armour push, I should put back to the line of the river Beas. I was aghast at this suggestion and said that since it was a tactical order, he had to come to the front with me to give it, or else he had to issue an operational instruction, as is the custom in the army.

Next morning, Lt. Gen. Harbaksh Singh met the COAS at the airfield at Ambala. In the operations room, they had a very heated discussion. Harbaksh Singh stood his ground and made it quite clear that if the COAS wanted to give a tactical order, he would have come to the front, and only then he would decide whether the tactical order should be carried out or not. After that frank exchange, the COAS left for Delhi after lunch in a much better mood. At that stage, the crucial battle was being fought around Assal Uttar.

That explains Chavan's entry: *COAS met in the evening briefing meeting. His visit to forward areas has done him good. He was more certain of himself.*

September 11, 1965

Morning meeting gave some hopeful and encouraging glimpse of the situation on the front.

Had discussions in the presence of the PM with CNS (Admiral S.M.S. Nanda). Necessary orders were given.

EEC was a general rambling affair. Important decision of giving 2/3 of salary as pension for 7 years to the families of those who are killed in action was taken.

News came through COAS that we had a good day's bag at Kasur (Lahore Sector): 17 tanks in that.

Party meeting in the evening. I gave them this news and there was all joy for it.

At the morning meeting Chavan reviewed the progress on the Sialkot front. The important towns and communications centers of India and Pakistan, Jammu and Sialkot respectively, are on either side of the border. The terrain on the Pakistani side is flat with no major obstacles to tanks approaching from the north on the Samba-Sialkot axis. An alternative approach for the Indians was from Gurdaspur. An offensive from that direction would however require crossing the Ravi. General Chaudhuri had opted to strike from the north on the Samba-Sialkot axis so that the 1 Armoured Division could be utilized to the maximum effect. Surprise being most important, it was decided to induct troops into the operational areas at the last moment possible.

September 12, 1965

U Thant has come today. Meet PM at 4 p.m.

Morning meeting—some further programme of Sialkot was given.

D.P. Dhar of Kashmir came to see me and gave his views on the whole situation.

CAS was given O.K. for Peshawar. When he (Air Marshal Arjan Singh) is asked to go ahead on a new task, CAS even walks as a dancing bird. A real fighting Sikh! And yet how soft and gentle.

Meeting with PM at 7 p.m. He told details to me and Sardarji (Swaran Singh, the Foreign Minister) of his talks with U Thant.

Military Operations

Operation Riddle launched on 6 September, envisaged a simultaneous assault by XI Corps in the Lahore Sector and I Corps in the Sialkot Sector with 6, 14, 26 Divisions and 1 Armoured Division.

Lt. Gen. Harbaksh Singh, the GOC Western Command, who had from the outset pressed to cross the international border and advancing up to the Ichhogil canal, had planned to keep the additional force, including the first armoured division in reserve. After securing the Ichhogil canal, he wanted to launch this reserve force against Sialkot, crossing the river Ravi in the area of Nainakot. Since the area was in the Indian territory, he had planned to put up a temporary bridge over Ravi but the COAS had other plans which he did not share with Lt. Gen. Harbaksh Singh. He had planned an attack in the direction of Samba, leaving no reserves in Punjab. This greatly upset the plan prepared by the GOC Western Command.

The aim of opening the second front was to draw enemy forces away Chhamb-Akhnur and Khem Karan-Amritsar zones. The task was to be performed by I Corps under command of Lt. Gen. P.O. Dunn. 6 Mountain Division was under Maj. Gen. S.K. Korla and 1 Armoured Division under Maj. Gen. Rajinder Singh 'Sparrow', MVC. Maj. Gen. Sparrow was senior in service to Dunn and that was to lead to command and control problems. It would be further complicated by Lt. Gen. Harbakash Singh being more or less kept away from actual conduct of I Corps operations.

6 Mountain Division and 26 Infantry Division moved forward on the night of 7/8 September and safeguarded the two flanks in order to allow the I Armoured Corps to launch its lightening strike towards Phillora. The idea was to establish a 'bridge head' by a Brigade of 14 Infantry Division to serve as a spring-board for launching main striking element, namely the 1 Armoured Division. Simultaneously, 26 Infantry Division would attack Sialkot town frontally.

As mentioned earlier, there was a delay of forty-eight hours in the launching of the 1 Corps operation. On 8 September, 1 Armoured Division broke out of the bridge-head punctually at 6 a.m. But the 43 lorried Infantry Group, under Sparrow, was grounded to a halt in a vast quagmire created by heavy shower of rain the previous day. The armoured division which was supposed to penetrate deep and to the rear of Sialkot had only advanced four miles after breakout from the bridge-head, when there was a very scanty armour opposition ranged against them and a great opportunity had been lost.

After initial melee on the 8th of September, 1 Armoured Division had taken shelter behind village Phillora for the next three days. During that time the Pakistani Ace Armoured

Division of Pattons could be ferried by railway, via Lahore to the Sialkot Sector. 1 Armoured Division thus now faced Pattons. Tardiness in launching attack greatly upset Lt. Gen. Harbaksh Singh and he took the GOC 1 Corps to task, on telephone, for not getting the Armoured Division going. When he was told that the Corps Commander had received instructions from Gen. Chaudhuri, over the telephone not to stick his head out too much forward, Lt. Gen. Harbaksh Singh remonstrated with the COAS, telling him that he had no business to give tactical instructions to the 1 Corps Commander. According to Lt. Gen. Harbaksh Singh, the COAS apologised for this.

Although the COAS's plan met with initial success, there was not enough time before the ceasefire came into effect on midnight of 22/23 September for it to develop its operations fully. According to Lt. Gen. Harbaksh Singh, because of the mess in handling forces by the GOC 1 Corps, Chhawinda could not be captured, in spite of many attempts made by us, incurring heavy casualties till the ceasefire came into effect.

The fighting in the Sialkot Sector had been envisaged essentially as a battle between the armoured forces of the two sides. 1 Armoured brigade had crossed the border and advanced along the Sabapir-Chobara-Phillora axis. After two night's break in engagement, by the midnight of 10/11 September, two brigades of the 1 Armoured Division had assembled for a frontal assault on Phillora.

In a hard fought battle, where hundred of tanks engaged in a slogging match, Pakistan lost over 50 tanks that day. There were heavy casualties on both sides. A local pincer movement by India's Armoured Regiments (4 and 17 Horse), had succeeded in isolating enemy armour in Phillora, threatening it with destruction. The enemy chose to vacate Phillora and remained on the defensive, making no attempt to wrest initiative or upset the Indian plan.

The battle for Phillora had been an exhausting one. The total gain from advance was of 5 kilometres from the Rurki Kalan area. The heavy tank losses had left the Pakistan forces unbalanced and shaken. Maj. Gen. Sparrow pulled back his 1 Armoured Division for rest on the night of 12/13 September. His mind was set on Chhawinda which he planned to storm frontally. It was considered essential to protect the right flank of the projected attack on Chhawinda against the enemy interference from Sialkot. For that purpose, the 6 Division was ordered to capture Pagowal cross-roads. By 7 a.m. of 13 September, that task had been accomplished.

At the time as the above operations, Pakistan troops were active against Phillora on 13 September. But all these attacks were beaten back.

Battle for Chhawinda

By the morning of 12 September, Pakistan was on the defensive in Sialkot Sector. The hasty attack for the capture of Khem Karan had been costly. Pak had started the war with a cocky confidence in the superiority of the Patton tanks over the tanks in the Indian Army. The destruction of 4 Cavalry on 10 September in the Khem Karan Battle and the loss of another regiment worth of Pattons in the Battle of Phillora on 11 September must have unnerved the Pak armour commanders and their high command.

4 Mountain Division had effected a crippling blow on the enemy. For Lt. Gen. Harbaksh Singh, the Army Commander, this was an exhilarating moment, especially as the Corps Commander and the COAS had expressed doubts on the outcome of the battle of Assal Uttar. His enthusiasm and ambition to achieve another great victory led almost to a disaster in the Khem Karan Sector.

On 12 and 13 September, both sides were busy and licking their wounds, preparatory for further action. During the past two days, 12/13 September, the Indians had made significant advances in two other sectors. In the Haji Pir bulge area, the Indian troops from Poonch had linked up with those in Haji Pir and gained a large chunk of POK area. In the far off Barmer Sector of Rajasthan, India had launched an offensive intended to tie down the Pakistan Division in that area.

Chavan had given the *go ahead* to the CAS to launch an attack on Peshawar. The mission was successfully carried out on the night of 13/14 September.

The Stupid Incident

10

By the evening of 11 September, it was obvious that Pakistan had suffered a major reverse and would not be in a position to carry out any offensive action in the Khem Karan Sector. However, they were strong enough to defend themselves and had taken strong defensive positions around Khem Karan town, extending their defences to either flank. Although this was known, the Indian commanders, flushed with the success of the Assal Uttar tank battle, decided hastily to undertake a task on the night of 11/12 September that would end up in the massacre of many troops and loss of face.

After the Pakistan rout in Assal Uttar, it was planned that an infantry battalion under direct Command of 4 Mountain Division would carry out night infiltration into Khem Karan, passing through eastern suburbs. The battalion was to support 7 Brigade attack, by firing on the enemy from behind its lines, thus creating panic amongst the enemy troops and facilitating the capture of Khem Karan town. The success of the operation depended on the infiltration and the battalion's subsequent role. GOC 4 Mountain Division was sounded to undertake the operation but he expressed his inability to find troops from within his Division. Although a battalion from nearby located brigade could have been entrusted the task, between the Army Commander, the Corps and the 4 Mountain Division Commanders, it was agreed that 4 Sikh Battalion which had fought valiantly the previous night should undertake the task.

In taking that decision, Lt. Gen. Harbaksh Singh, who was also the Colonel of the Sikh Regiment, was motivated to seek valour and honour for the Sikh Regiment. 12th September was for 4 Sikh Battle Honour Saragarhi Day. On that day in

1897, a small band of 21 men of 4 Sikh under Havildar Ishar Singh had created a saga of unsurpassed gallantry and self-sacrifice in the call of duty, when under attack from about 20,000 Orazai and Afridi tribesmen, each and every one of them died fighting the assaulting hordes. As a befitting and rare gesture, all the twenty-two, including the Safai Karamchari, were posthumously awarded Indian Order of Merit (IOM), the highest gallantry award given to Indian ranks those days. Lt. Gen. Harbaksh must have felt that he, as Colonel Commandant of the Sikh Regiment, had been presented a God-sent opportunity to give 4 Sikhs a chance of adding another feather to the Saragarhi Saga.

He sent for Lt. Colonel Anant Singh, Commanding Officer of 4 Sikh, to ask him personally if he would be willing to undertake the arduous task. Face-to-face with his Colonel Commandant and the Army Commander, Anant Singh accepted the challenge without even mentioning that he and his men had no sleep for two previous nights and in their attack on Barki, his battalion had suffered nearly 150 casualties. 12 September, the Saragarhi Day, thus became inexorably linked with the operation. This led to a great disaster.

7 Mountain Brigade, earmarked to launch the operation from the front, was led by Brigadier Sidhu, who found that neither the 4 Sikh nor the 2 Mahar Regiments had seen the ground. He proposed postponing the operation by 24 hours. Major Gen. Gurubax Singh, GOC, 4 Mountain Division, insisted that as decided by the army commander, the operation had to take place during the night of 11/12th September. No postponement was possible as the 12 September was the Saragarhi Day. Having exhausted all avenues to obtain postponement, Lt. Col. Anant undertook to do his best and with a depleted strength of around 300, 4 Sikh undertook its night march on man-pack basis along the railway track at midnight. Along the way, they shed the anti-tank guns which were delaying their move. The Signal detachment also separated from the marching unit during the night and they had no means of communication with anyone. At about 4.45 a.m. on 12th September, they could harbour in tall crops, believing it to be near Khem Karan. Unknown to 4 Sikh, they were

sharing the ground with a Pak tank unit. In the morning Pakistani troops were surprised to find the Sikhs. They jumped into their tanks and firing machine guns rounded up the Sikh troops. Lt. Col. Anant Singh with 126 others who were taken prisoners, twenty were killed. The unit that had covered itself with glory the previous night came suddenly to an ignoble end.

Next morning when 2 Mahar troops approached the Khem Karan distributary, they were attacked by the PAF repeatedly. 2 Mahar fell back after suffering heavy casualty. Despite subsequent efforts, their attack towards Khem Karan failed. They lost 11 tanks and 3 officers, 2 JCOs and 45 jawans while 3 officers, 4 JCOs and 83 jawans were wounded. Later, Brigadier Sidhu was brought down in rank for the failure of the attack.

Chavan learnt of the carnage next day and recorded on 13 September: *The stupid incident (of) Lt. Col. Anant and 300 Sikhs took place yesterday.* Later, after full facts were found out, it was clear that it was overzealous army commander who had pushed tired, unprepared and ill equipped troops to a task that led to disaster. Incidentally, Harbaksh Singh hardly mentions his own role in this tragedy in his memoirs.

On page 355 of *A Soldier Remembers*, he states that he had left it to the GOC, 4 Division, to plan the operation. So far as Lt. Col. Anant Singh is concerned, he states, "What was not realised at that time was the fact that 4 Sikh had, for the capture of Barki, spent the previous two nights without any sleep and had besides, suffered heavy casualties during the operation. But their Commanding Officer, Lt. Col. Anant Singh, whom I had sent for to ask if he could undertake this hazardous operation, was a fine soldier that not even once did he raise the question of fatigue among his men, nor of the number of casualties that had already suffered. He, on the other hand, undertook the night operation planned by General Officer Commanding, 4 Division, on the same night, that is, the 11th of September."

The *Stupid Incident* was successfully kept out of the news at that time.

Stepping Up of Pressure 11

September 13, 1965

EEC at 9 a.m. U Thant's proposals were placed before us. He wants a final reply by 15 (September) morning. We, particularly, I and TTK (Krishnamachari), pressed for conditional acceptance. But no final view could emerge.

Morning meeting: Steady progress everywhere. The stupid incident (of) Lt. Col. Anant and 300 Sikhs took place yesterday.

Lunch with President for U Thant.

4 p.m. Executive of the Congress party in Parliament daily briefing—very critical of peace proposals.

6.30 p.m. ECC again. General view that emerged was that we should accept the proposal of cessation of hostilities.

But made our position clear on the following two points:

(1) The new pockets occupied in Kashmir should not be given up as they were essential for preventing infiltration and;

(2) Kashmir is no longer a problem of political negotiations as far as India was concerned.

PM's dinner in U Thant's honour was a quiet peaceful affair.

September 14, 1965

Morning meeting—As usual 'nothing special' report was given by COAS.

This is rather unusual. I must find out why things are not moving. I will have to look into it today and tomorrow.

CAS gave a report of the visit to Peshawar.

Reports of Pak attacks on Barrackpore and Agartala came. CAS was keen that we give him permission to start things in East Pakistan. I had told him to wait for a day. One more incident and he is free to go ahead.

Had a talk with CNS about his plans. He is rather too keen to do something. I had to restrain him.

Pradhan (the Author) came to see me. He has just returned from Geneva. He has offered his services. I liked it.

In the noon, leaders of the Opposition were called by the PM and ECC (and) Executive Committee (of the Congress Party in Parliament) also endorsed the same.

At 4 p.m. ECC met again. Here the PM produced a different draft than the one that was shown yesterday (Chavan has added in Marathi: I did not like this sleight of hand). I felt that the draft was too long and vague. I said so. COAS suggested some changes.

At 5 p.m. I had discussion with U Thant for about 45 minutes in my office. Events since 5 August were recounted and I put across my point of view. Defence secretary and the COAS were present.

September 15, 1965

ECC to consider the reply to U Thant. It was decided after some discussion to reply in a more agreeable way. But it is strange that UThant has again equated both India and Pakistan.

Met Executive at 4 p.m.—had a usual type of discussion. I gave them some information on the happenings on the front.

ECC meeting again at 5 p.m. U Thant has sent another proposal, offering his own mediation. This proposal surprised even PM. Does it mean that U Thant expected the failure of the proposal of ceasefire?

The whole affair looked like a mechanical process.

PM authorised the announcement to be broadcast that war efforts will continue unabated.

At 6 p.m. met Chiefs of Staff. I informed them of the results of the ECC and asked them to take a close review of their strategies. Both of them (COAS and CAS) would go in forward areas tomorrow for discussions.

September 16, 1965

No morning meeting today. Went straight to Lok Sabha. PM made a statement on U Thant talks and its results. It was very well received in the House. All the opposition party leaders supported the stand of government. Only Dr. Ram Manohar Lohia, in his own typical way said: "We are behind the army. We are not behind the government—but on its side."

It was a heartening sight to see all parties united on a major national issue.

At 12.45 I called Lt. Gen. Kumarmangalam (the Adjutant General) for some discussion. We took a review of what happened in the last week. We both agreed that 8th-9th September were critical days. At one point, things looked rather gloomy. Stubborn attitude both in HQ (Army) and at Western Command saved the situation. At Army HQ someone at top mentioned withdrawal to Beas (river). But fortunately it was immediately scotched.

Gen. K. (Kumarmangalam) feels that one more major and serious effect should be expected on the part of Pakistan. Where? Sialkot—he thought.

At 6 pm. COAS (and) CAS came and reported the gist of their impressions of forward areas. I have insisted today to break the stalemate in front.

Must do something that will put tremendous pressure on (President) Ayub.

On 16 September there was no morning meeting as both the COAS and CAS had gone to the forward areas as directed by the defence minister. Chavan had a longish talk with the adjutant general on the military operations. He trusted Lt. Gen. Kumarmangalam's judgment.

At that stage, Chavan was eager to end the stalemate in the Sialkot Sector. He knew that the ceasefire was imminent. Also, he could not take the Chinese threats lightly.

Unfortunately, the Pakistanis had recaptured Phillora and the Indian troops could not make decisive moves on Chhawinda. The good news however was that in several skirmishes the Indians had destroyed as many as 240 Pakistani tanks.

Military Operations

There was very little activity on the Sialkot front. That had intrigued the defence minister. He felt that the *nothing special* reported by the COAS at the morning meeting was rather unusual. He had decided to find out *why things are not moving*.

Following stalemate on the front after heavy fighting on 14 September, Indian commanders decided to re-shuffle the available forces and drew fresh plans for the capture of Chhawinda.

Operation on the Sialkot front were disappointing and somewhat frustrating for both sides who were gearing up for the battle of Chhawinda. Having failed to win the offensive battle in Khem Karan on 10 September, Pak decided not to lose the defensive battle at Chhawinda. On the other hand, the victory at Phillora had raised the confidence and fighting spirit of the Indian tank men which received a big boost after news of the success at Assal Uttar came in. On 13 September, GOC I Corps decided to employ 1 Armoured Division for the capture of Chhawinda.

The battle started at first light on 14 September. There was fierce fighting that lasted throughout the day. It was a day of mutual attrition and disappointment. The battle of Chhawinda would last several days. The lull in fighting and certain lack of initiative by the Indian commanders had enabled Pakistani troops to reinforce strong defences in that sector.

Another attack on Chhawinda was scheduled to commence on the 17/18 September. It was, however, postponed for 24 hours. The assault was finally launched on the night of 18/19 September.

Assault had a bad beginning. With the loss of surprise, our troops were subjected to intense bombardment. Two brigades

(36 and 58) made a spirited assault but lack of fire support spelt doom for the attack. Short of tanks, the infantry unit disintegrated and troops disappeared in the surrounding darkness. The brigade and battalion commander made desperate attempt to collect their commands, but failed. During the battle of Chhawinda, both sides had endeavored to tie down maximum number of each other troops in areas away from Chhawinda. In hard-fought battles, both the sides sustained heavy losses. With the news of the impending ceasefire, a stalemate continued on the Sialkot Sector.

Only one *final* battle was being planned by both adversaries.

Retreat to the Beas

12

Chavan's entry on 16 September that, *at Army HQ someone at top mentioned withdrawal to Beas (river). But fortunately it was scotched,* has a story that came out much later. Lt. Gen. Harbaksh Singh, the Western Army Commander, has recounted that in his memoirs. The controversy in the Indian army circles centered around: whether a suggestion, namely withdrawal to the Beas, was made at all by General Chaudhuri?

Briefly, the origin of the controversy lay in the strategy discussions after the 1962 India-China conflict. Pakistan's acquisition of modern weapons from the United States had tilted the military balance in favour of Pakistan. There were two schools of thought for framing India's defence strategy in the Punjab. One school favoured defending the border, while the second advocated a defence line along the Beas river. Taking into account Pakistan's superiority in armour and fire power, the former school felt that a major battle in the west of the Beas would end in the destruction of the Indian army and thereafter allow the enemy forces to push to the gates of Delhi without much resistance. They believed that the defence potential of the Beas should be utilized to hold any Pakistani onslaught. It seems General Chaudhuri was also inclined towards this view.

General Chaudhuri had been under great mental strain since 6 September. Despite his known inclination to make the Beas defence line, he had opted for the Ichhogil canal. Progress on that front had been somewhat tardy and naturally that must have caused him great anxiety. As observed by Chavan in his entry on 9 September, he had found the COAS *somewhat uncertain of himself*. Probably at that time Chaudhuri might have mentioned option for the defence line along the east bank of the Beas.

In the light of this background, the controversy surfaced out of the account of discussion that General Chaudhuri had with Lt. Gen. Harbaksh Singh, the Army Commander, during his visit to Ambala on 10 September. On that day, the situation on the Khem Karan-Kasur Sector had reached a critical stage. Developments in the 4 Mountain Division operations were also causing concern. The COAS feared that the *worst night happen*. During the COAS's discussions with the Army Commander some unpleasant words had been exchanged between the two.

Chavan's entry that *someone at top mentioned withdrawal to the Beas*, lends credence to what had been talked about. I have, however, no doubt that Chavan must have ruled out any such proposal because as a politician, Chavan could not countenance any such withdrawal. Events of 1962 were still fresh and he knew that although in November 1962 the Indian troops' withdrawal to the foothills of Assam could be justified as sound tactical move, it was rightly perceived as a rout because of panicky behaviour of the commanders in the field and that had led to ouster of Krishna Menon. Aware of that background and the mood of the Parliament, Defence Minister Chavan could not countenance any withdrawal.

As a matter of fact, at that stage of the conflict, Chavan was eager to end the stalemate in the Sialkot Sector. He knew that the ceasefire was imminent. Also, he could not take the Chinese threats lightly. Unfortunately, the Pakistanis had recaptured Phillora and the Indian troops could not make decisive moves on Chhawinda. The good news however was that in several skirmishes the Indians had destroyed as many as 240 Pakistani tanks.

For several years after the war, in army circles, the subject whether Gen. Chaudhuri made any suggestion to withdraw was hotly debated. He was not a particularly popular person and attracted criticism because of his swagger and superiority attitude towards his colleagues. Many must have found it convenient to attack him on grounds of professional incompetence to make such a suggestion at the height of battles shaping in Assal Uttar and Khem Karan Sectors. The author has no doubt that Chaudhuri must have articulated on the subject—if not actually made such a suggestion to Chavan. Evidence of that was found in Gen. Chaudhuri's correspondence* with Chavan while he was India's High Commissioner to Canada.

In 1967 Lt. Gen. B.M. Kaul was about to publish his memoirs, "The Untold Story". Chaudhuri got to know that in that book, Kaul had made critical assessment of Chaudhuri's army career and especially about his conduct of the 1965 War. On learning that on 31st January 1967, Chaudhuri wrote to Chavan about the portion that he considered defamatory and Chavan replied to him on 29th February 1967 stating: "I quite appreciate your concern about portion of the book which you consider defamatory to you. I can assure you that, if the need arises, I shall say something to put the record straight. We shall discuss this matter when you come to Delhi."

To be fair to B.M. Kaul, he did criticize Gen. J.N. Chaudhuri and his track record in the army, but he wrote about the suggestion without mentioning the Beas. He wrote, "His 'prize' effort was to have asked one of his senior commanders, whilst the battle of Khem Karan was still in progress, on 9/10 September, to take up an alternative position, several miles in the rear which would have meant giving up some well-known and vital places in the areas (if he had been obeyed, India would have been in a desperate situation. But thanks to Lt. Gens. Harbaksh Singh and Dhillon's grit, we were saved from the plight)" (page 478 of *The Untold Story*).

Chavan's Diary has confirmed that a suggestion to retreat to the Beas was made. The fact that Lt. Gen. Kumarmangalam mentioned that to Chavan and he recorded that "*someone at top made suggestion to withdrawal to the Beas*", leaves no doubt that the suggestion could have been made only by the COAS. Lt. Gen. Harbaksh Singh's account is truthful.

---

*Chavan's papers in Venutai Chavan Smarak Library, Karad.

The Chinese Checkers 13

September 17, 1965

I was woken up from sleep at 6 a.m. to be told about the Chinese severe note amounting to ultimatum to dismantle within three days the construction on Chinese territory near Sikkim's border. It was confirmed by 6.30 a.m. by AIR news.

ECC at 9 a.m. at prime minister's house to consider Chinese note. Meeting lasted nearly 2 hours.

It was decided to agree to the joint inspection and send an early reply. But the general feeling was that (the) Chinese would not accept this proposal. It was just an excuse to start trouble for India in support of Pakistan. The main political purpose seems to be to see that Pakistan does not get weak so as to accept ceasefire proposal under the pressure of USA and Russia. Militarily to see that pressure on Pakistan is relieved and also to give military support to Kashmir LOC (Line of Actual Control).

Prime minister made a statement in Parliament at 3.30 p.m. It was soberly received.

First news of the movement of Chinese army started coming in.

Tuting in Siang Division of NEFA and Chhamb Valley (Sikkim/Bhutan) were mentioned.

Had a long talk with COAS about Chinese threat and our position in different places.

Prime minister called in the evening. He was in a mood to talk. We discussed in great length the Chinese threat.

The People's Republic of China had been carefully monitoring the outcome of the conflict. On 8 September, when the Pakistani armoured offensive was beginning in Punjab, the Chinese made the first of a series of threats against India. In a formal note, China accused India of violating the Sikkim border on several occasions during July and August. Demanding a halt to further provocations the note warned that "India must bear the responsibility for all the consequences arising therefrom."

While a large-scale Chinese attack was not anticipated, Chavan felt that China would launch some kind of diversionary action, in order to relieve pressure on Pakistan and derive maximum diplomatic gain at minimum risk. In that context, the movement of Chinese troops in NEFA was ominous.

September 18, 1965

At 11.30 (a.m.), had a two-hour discussion in the prime minister's room in South Block when both Chiefs of Staff (Chief of Army Staff Gen. Chaudhuri and Air Marshal Arjan Singh), the Cabinet Secretary, Home Secretary, Defence Secretary and L.K. Jha, were present. General review of our objective was taken. Supply position was considered. Some early decision was necessary in Chhamb Sector. This was necessary (for) both political and military reasons. I stressed this point. COAS will look into this.

This meeting was necessary to clear the minds. USA, USSR and UK were to be approached.

Apparently the day was devoted to analysing the Chinese intentions. Their threat could not be taken lightly. Diplomatic moves had already been initiated to seek help from the UK, the USSR and the USA. At the same time there was much behind-the-scene activity in the United Nations Security Council. U Thant had returned to New York and the delegates had begun working on a new resolution for peace on the subcontinent.

September 19, 1965

(1) *Morning and evening meetings as usual to take review with the Chiefs of Staff.*

(2) *I broadcast my speech. It was well-received. Nandaji (Gulzarilal Nanda, the Home Minister), and Manubhai (Shah, the Commerce Minister) telephoned to say (that) they liked it much.*

Baba (More, Y.B. Chavan's brother-in-law) phoned from Bombay to say the same. It is a comfortable feeling to know that your family members like what you do or say.

(3) *Sad news of the death of CM (Chief Minister) Gujarat Balwantrai Mehta came at 10.30 p.m. (previous night). It was shocking news. He died in air accident.*

China's "deadline" was due to expire that day. Chavan's broadcast was intended to reassure the nation that the Indian troops were ready to face the Chinese threat.

Captured weapons and ammunitions being shown to Defence Minister

Captured weapons and ammunitions being shown to Defence Minister

Defence Minister with Air Officers and Gnat that shot down Pakistan's F-104

Y.B. Chavan addressing Army Officers and Jawans

Defence Minister visiting Front with COAS

Y.B. Chavan with Jawans

Pak's Patton Tanks captured in Khemkaran Sector

At dinner hosted for the Chiefs: (left to right) Air-Marshal Arjan Singh, Gen. J.N. Chaudhuri, C. Subramaniam, Admiral D.S. Soman

PART - II : **UN & OTHER DIPLOMATIC INTERVENTIONS**

NOTE: For convenience, extracts of the Diary have been reproduced so that readers do not have to refer to entries made in PART I.

Last Phase

14

September 20, 1965

Early morning by 5 a.m., I was woken by shrill ring of phone by my bedside, PVR (P.V.R. Rao, the Defence Secretary) was speaking. He was ringing to tell me that further information had come about Balwantbhai (Mehta's) air accident. It was not an accident but was shot down by Pakistani fighter planes near Bhuj. It was surprising that the plane went off the track nearly by 50 miles between Ahmedabad-Mithapur. I hate these Pakistanis. It was the most dastardly attack on non-military and a tiny plane. Balwantbhai has died a martyr's death.

In my meeting with the Chiefs of Staff, I mentioned to them about the possibility of ceasefire as Security Council resolution was expected any time. What was their view?

COAS told me that he had prepared an assessment from (the) military point of view and he would show it to me later.

He came back alone with the assessment. His thesis was that the twin purpose of (1) doing damage to the war potential and military machine of Pakistan and (2) defeating the purpose and plan of Pakistan to decide the Kashmir issue by military strength were achieved. We are on top of the situation (and) if we agree to the ceasefire now, army would support it. The respite we will get will be good to put things right as far as supplies were concerned. Politically, we were completely isolated. To reject ceasefire would be in the long run militarily also unwise. China's game is to continue (the) struggle so that they can fish in the troubled waters.

I think it is good that the military and political thinking was moving in the same direction.

Chinese extended their ultimatum by three days. Very clever people.

ECC (met) in the evening. Security Council Resolution had come by this time ordering ceasefire by the morning of 22nd. ECC generally discussed and adjourned to meet next day.

When I was in the Chiefs of Staff meeting at 6 p.m. message came that I should meet prime minister with defence secretary and chief of army staff. L.K. Jha was present. We met at 7 p.m. in prime minister's office.

After some preliminary discussion about the military point of view, it was agreed that prime minister should send to U Thant, through G. Parthasarthy (India's Permanent Representative to the UN) (a message) confirming our willingness to order simple ceasefire if Pakistan is agreeable.

Army commanders on both the sides had veered round to ending the war. Pakistan had nearly reached the end of her tether. While India had greater reserves, the COAS, after careful assessment of the situation on the ground, came to the conclusion that India's main objectives had been achieved. The army was on top of the situation and ready to unreservedly support the simple ceasefire. This would also deflect the Chinese threat.

India had occupied the Haji Pir bulge and captured territory in Tithwal and Kargil in Jammu and Kashmir as well as strips of land on the Lahore and the Sialkot Sectors. Pakistan had made gains in Chhamb and Khem Karan. In terms of area, India had captured about 720 square miles of Pakistan held about 400 square miles of Indian territory.

The prime minister, after a high-level review, accepted the proposal and the theatre of operations shifted to the United Nations in New York. The Chinese had watered down their threat by unilaterally announcing the extension of the time limit by 72 hours, on expiration of the original deadline. China thus attempted to extract the last ounce of profit from the situation.

Situation on Front

Gen. Chaudhuri had launched 1 Corps with high hopes of decisive results in the Sialkot Sector. The pressure to bring about ceasefire between India and Pakistan had been mounting since middle of September and the battles of Chhawinda, Khem Karan and Dograi were fought under the shadow of impending ceasefire. Gen. Chaudhuri expecting a big victory on the Chhawinda front urged the Indian Government to avoid a ceasefire at such a crucial stage of war. One final battle for Dograi was taking shape at that very moment.

Dograi—The Final Battle

It was becoming apparent by then that neither side could achieve a decisive victory swaying the fortunes of war in the immediate future. The war was slipping towards a long-term battle of attrition where the commanders on both sides were waging war for the sake of it. Both sides felt that if one agreed to stop fighting, the other side would enlarge its demands as the price of peace. Thus, commanders on both sides were looking for a fitting battle victory before agreeing to ceasefire. At that stage, 11 Corps was gearing itself for launching an offensive. Lt. Gen. Dhillon had planned to reach the Ichhogil canal in 15 Division Sector and also to liberate Khem Karan, while pursuing operations to clear the Pakistanis from the east of the Ichhogil canal in the Bari Doab Sector.

Dograi, a medium size township, had developed astride the G.T. Road to the east of the Ichhogil canal since partition. The old village was some distance away from the road. Since the vacation of Dograi on 6 September, 11 Corps had been pushing 15 Division to reach the east bank of the Ichhogil canal. Capture of Dograi had been planned, but somehow had failed to fructify under pressure of events.

Phase 1 of the attack was launched astride the G.T. Road at 23:30 hours on 21 September after a heavy preliminary artillery and mortar bombardment. The squadron of 14 Horse joined in with direct fire at night. The attack did not make progress due to intense enemy artillery, mortar and machine gun fire. Despite exhortations from the brigade commander, the troops failed to make progress. The battle continued with full ferocity, indirectly helping 3 Jat in achieving surprise, as the enemy believed that the whole of the Indian brigade was involved in the attack on Milestone 13 area. Under cover of the noise of battle and artillery fire from both sides, 3 Jat reached their forward assembly area by about 00:45 hours on 22 September without detection by the enemy. At this stage, they learnt about the failure of Phase 1.

3 Jat launched the attack on Dograi at 01:30 hours on 22 September after the prearranged artillery bombardment. The firing around Milestone 13 went on as before. The enemy had no inkling that 3 Jat was poised to hit them from the northern flank. So the attack came as a complete surprise to the defenders of Dograi. After a stiff fight in the built-up area, Dograi was in 3 Jat hands by about 03:30 hours on 22 September. Both sides suffered heavy casualties in the bitter struggle. 3 Jat had 4 officers and 59 other ranks killed, while 6 officers, 5 JCOs and 142 other ranks were wounded. A total of 300 enemy dead was counted and about 100 were taken prisoners, including Lt. Col. Golewala, Commanding Officer of 16 Punjab and his affiliated battery commander.

After first light, 13 Punjab pressed forward supported by a squadron of 14 Horse, and linked up with 3 Jat in Dograi by about 07:30 hours. A number of Pakistanis from the Milestone 13 area tried to flee, unaware of the presence of 3 Jat in Dograi. Most of them were taken prisoner or shot. Small parties of the enemy kept on walking into the Dograi area from the western side of the Ichhogil to end up as prisoners. The total Indian casualties in the Dograi battle, including 3 Jat were, 5 officers and 72 other ranks killed, while 10 Officers, 7 JCOs and 222 other ranks were wounded. 3 Jat captured 13 tanks, 13 vehicles, 23 RCL guns, 35 MMGs and the large amount of other weapons and ammunition. Victory was achieved by the grit and determination of under the indomitable spirit of its commanding officer, Lt. Col. (later Brigadier) Desmond E. Hyde who had been awarded the MVC on 12 September for his outstanding qualities of leadership during the first week of the war.

The battle of Dograi was fought under the shadow of the impending ceasefire. Despite Pakistan initiating the war, it was India that carried the fighting over to Pak territory, showing Pakistani operational capabilities in a poor light to the world at large. That was a finale' to a war that Pakistan initiated. A large number of men laid down their lives in those final hours, not knowing that the ceasefire was about to take place.

By 21 September, Indian attacks against Pakistan's prepared defences at Chhawinda in the Khem Karan Sector had failed. Dograi, in Sialkot Sector, with heavy loss of life, was our only success. That was enough for Indian commanders to signal an end to the military operations. Upon that, the COAS and the GOC, Western Command, agreed that we could now accept ceasefire.

By that time, India had occupied the Haji Pir bulge and captured territory in Tithwal and Kargil in J&K as well as strips of land in the Lahore and Sialkot areas. Pakistan had made gains in Chhamb and Khem Karan Sectors. India had captured about 720 square miles of Pak territory, including about 150 square miles in the Barmer area, while Pakistan held about 400 square miles of Indian territory. Pakistan claimed possession additionally of a considerable strip of territory along the periphery of the Rajasthan border. In a smart move, Pak Desert Rangers had secured a number of posts along the border during the night of 22/23 September in a pre-ceasefire offensive.

September 21, 1965

This was a fast-moving day. Morning brought the news of China's firing in Nathula (Sikkim) and other places Three days' extension was just a bluff. Our troops were ordered to reply to the fire, if fired upon and to take defensive positions if a major attack came.

(1) *ECC met. Prime minister told them about the message already sent to U Thant. ECC agreed without much discussion.*

(2) *Party executive met and endorsed prime minister's action with enthusiasm.*

(3) *All Party leaders met. They thought that prime minister's action of sending the message to U Thant a diplomatic and wise move.*

Confirmation came that Balwantbhai (Mehta's) plane was shot down by (a) Pakistani plane.

News came in the evening that Bhutto (Foreign Minister) left Pakistan on way to New York to address the Security Council.

I think he will bark and bark there and ultimately agree to the ceasefire.

As anticipated, the Chinese threat disappeared in the next twenty-four hours. High level diplomacy and the war of words at the UN had begun. Bhutto, the Foreign Minister of Pakistan, was on his way to New York.

Both India and Pakistan accepted the ceasefire effective from 3.30 a.m. on 23 September.

September 22, 1965.

I was in bed at 5 a.m. when P.V.R. Rao phoned to tell me that Parthasarthy has phoned to say that (the) secretary general wants us to declare unilateral ceasefire. It was an absurd suggestion. I told him it is better that ECC meet to consider. I am dead opposed to such (a) suicidal thing.

8.30 (a.m.) ECC met. I put forward my point of view. ECC agreed. A message was sent to Parthasarthy.

After (the) morning meeting I got a message by 11 a.m. that Bhutto is addressing the Security Council and a rumour reached that he was asking for more time. I called COAS to consider the implication of such a move.

He came to me at 12 o'clock. Was with me for one hour. We were going into the pros and cons. CAS came and told me about air battle in the Kasur area—5 (planes) were shot down. We were in Khem Karan, etc.

By 12.45 p.m. message came through news agency that Bhutto has agreed to ceasefire. In the meanwhile, COAS came with draft instructions. Prime minister's word came that we all go to him and discuss. We showed the draft instructions to prime minister and he authorized its issue. It was 1.30 p.m.

Prime minister made a statement (in the parliament) at 3.30 p.m. It was well received.

4.30 p.m. ECC met. Prime minister made a short speech and congratulated COAS and CAS. We all felt proud.

Cabinet colleagues warmly congratulated me.

Army and air force have become now for us the symbols of our national pride and glory. A great day for me. A great day for Chaudhuri and Arjan Singh.

It was just then (that I) remembered a talk with Krishna Menon only a week ago. He told me that I depended too much on Chaudhuri and he is a general who will never fight. I told him that I disagreed with him. He was going by his personal dislikes. I have told him that from what I have seen of him (Chaudhuri) in the last 3 years, I am sure if it comes to vindicate the honour of (the) Indian army, Chaudhuri will fight. And today, I was vindicated in my judgment of the man. He fought and fought well.

Air Marshal Arjan Singh is a jewel of a person; quietly efficient and firm; unexcitable but a very able leader.

So the first round is over—where is the second round and when?

I have a feeling that this is the real beginning of trouble in this part of the world. How we utilize the respite that we are getting is going to decide the future of the country. The dangerous process of encirclement of India by hostile countries is complete. The leading powers of UNO, including USSR, are not with us on (the) Kashmir issue. We are tragically alone.

This is the achievement of our foreign policy. The issue (Kashmir) is basically political. Its solution will have to be political.

We have, with good luck, come out of it (the conflict) well. But if we try to make it again purely military, it will be a disastrous mistake. Unless we make quick and radically new moves to break the political isolation that we find ourselves in.

The ball is now in the political court again—where it should be—and not the military one.

I hope we have the vision and courage to accept this challenge to (our) political leadership.

On 20 September, the Security Council had adopted a unanimous resolution—with Jordan abstaining—demanding a ceasefire on the morning of 22 September and a subsequent withdrawal of all armed personnel to the position of 5 August. After this, as done, the Council promised to consider 'what steps could be taken to assist towards a settlement of the political problem underlying the conflict. The resolution called on all States to refrain from any action that might aggravate the situation in the area. This was a warning to Peking.

Bhutto, after indulging in last-minute dramatics in the Security Council, at the precise moment when the original UN deadline was to expire at 3 a.m. New York, time announced that President Ayub had ordered a ceasefire in the interest of international peace.

There was much jubilation all round. Gen. J.N. Chaudhuri and Air Marshal Arjan Singh were warmly congratulated by the prime minister. It was a great day for Chavan as well.

War & Diplomacy

15

Pakistani incursions in the Rann of Kutch in April 1965, had attracted the attention of international community to the possibility of armed conflict between India and Pakistan. At that time, the British Prime Minister, Harold Wilson, had made some proposals for a ceasefire. Lal Bahadur Shastri had stated in the Parliament on 28 April 1965, that India would be prepared to a peaceful settlement regarding Kutch provided a *status quo ante* is restored. He had also warned that 'if Pakistan discards reason and persists in its aggressive activities, the Indian Army will defend the country and it will decide its own strategy and the employment of its own manpower and equipment in the manner it deems best.

The British High Commissioners in India and Pakistan had persisted with their efforts and after intense diplomatic activity a ceasefire became effective on 1 July 1965. It was agreed that the border in this sector would be demarcated by a three-man tribunal. India nominated a Yugoslav, Pakistan an Iranian and the UN Secretary-General nominated a Swedish national as Chairman. The possibility of the escalation of the armed conflict was thus avoided with active intervention of the British Prime Minister and of the Secretary-General of the United Nations.

With this background, increasing infiltration by Pakistan across the Kashmir border and India's successful operation to flush them out, possibility of armed conflict was anticipated. U Thant, the Secretary-General of the UN, was being kept informed of the developments by General Robert H. Nimmo (an Australian), who headed the United Nations Military

Observer Group. He had kept the UN fully informed about the violations across the border and firing across the ceasefire line by Pakistani regular troops. At that stage, U Thant drafted a statement on Kashmir which would lay responsibility on Pakistan for the disturbance in Kashmir, and an advance copy of the statement was made available to the Government of India and Pakistan before placing the same before the Security Council. Pakistan raised serious objections. With a view to preserving the possibility of playing a mediating role in future, U Thant decided not to issue the proposed statement. Later, U Thant would play personally an important role in bringing about the ceasefire.

The Soviet Union was following the events with deep interest. It maintained its traditional stand that Kashmir was part of India and accepted that the disturbances in Kashmir had been created by infiltrators from Pakistan. The best policy at that time, according to the USSR, was for both the countries to resolve the dispute by peaceful means. USA was deeply involved in Vietnam and had decided to work through UN. China was watching the developments and would no doubt take a position at appropriate time and in keeping with its friendship with Pakistan.

This was the situation in the last week of August. General Nimmo was at the United Nations in New York to brief the Secretary-General about the situation arising from steady increase in infiltrations by Pakistan and the Indian forces crossing the ceasefire line in Uri Sector on 28 August 1965. By 31 August, the Secretary-General had completed his consultations with General Nimmo, who left New York the previous night, to return to his responsibilities in Kashmir.

By morning of 1 September, U Thant's report based on his consultations with General Nimmo was with the Foreign Secretary, C.S. Jha. In his Diary on 1 September, Chavan refers to that report, stating: *6.30 p.m. ECC (Emergency Committee of the Cabinet). C.S. Jha (the Foreign Secretary) read out U Thant's report.*

U Thant stated: "(there are) alarming reports indicating a steady escalation of the fighting in the air and on ground, involving regular army forces on both sides," and appealed to the leaders of the two warring nations to maintain peace.

By the morning of 2 September, diplomatic pressures were already building up. The external affairs ministry was preparing responses to the message from the Secretary-General of the UN. While diplomats were at work, Chavan's mind was on the situation on the battle ground. That is where his performance as defence minister was at test. Reports were not encouraging.

Immense diplomatic pressure was building up to restrain India from launching any counter-attack. In his appeal to the leaders of two warring nations, the Secretary-General called for peace. The British high commissioner had delivered a message from Harold Wilson making certain proposals. Chavan had noted in his Diary that: *I insisted on military advantages being maintained. Those UK proposals look like a trap.*

On 3 September, Chavan noted: *ECC at 9 p.m. Conditional acceptance (of U Thant's) was the proposal from E.A. Ministry.*

Significantly, President Johnson decided that the United States would not pressurize either side directly but instead rely on the UN for the time being.

On 4 September PM sent a detailed reply to U Thant, the UN Secretary-General, stating that: "Pakistan had launched a massive infiltration across the Ceasefire Line.... That aggression throws on us, a sovereign State, responsibilities for defence which is our right and duty to discharge.... Mr Secretary-General, you have appealed for peace and we greatly appreciate your anxiety and sincerity of your efforts.... I trust that, in the first instance, you will ascertain from Pakistan if it will accept responsibility for withdrawing not only its armed forces but also the infiltrators and for preventing further infiltration. This, in fact, we take it, is the basic assumption underlying your appeal."

PM also sent the Foreign Secretary, C.S. Jha, to New York to present India's case before the Security Council. In anticipation of military moves planned by Chavan with PM's full backing, it was decided that M.C. Chagla, the Education Minister and eminent jurist, should also proceed to New York.

In New Delhi, there was speculation about the 'next step'. US Ambassador, Chester Bowles, and UK High Commissioner, Mr Freeman, became active to press India to positively respond to U Thant's appeal. PM was waiting for the next move on the border and action of military significance to repel the Pakistani thrust in the Chhamb Sector, before taking any softer line. Chavan, knowing all this too well, was anxiously waiting to launch the bold move.

On diplomatic front, China was not to be left behind on. The Chinese Vice-Minister and Foreign Minister, Marshal Chen Yi, came on a visit to Pakistan. At the end of talks with Bhutto, he declared full support to Pakistan and for the struggle of freedom fighters in Kashmir.

On 5 September, Chavan noted:

ECC met twice 1 p.m. and 4.45 p.m. Reply to U Thant was finalized. Prime minister supported by most of us except Swaran Singh had taken unreasonably strong line.

That morning, Chavan spent several hours with the prime minister, assessing the discussions in the Security Council in New York and response to the Council's appeal for a ceasefire. Diplomatic pressures were already building up. Reports from the front were not encouraging.

At that stage, reports about the Security Council's meeting held on 4 September were received. The Council had noted that the Pakistan had committed the aggression; that Pakistan had violated the ceasefire terms and that Pakistan army had launched an open invasion on 1 September.

On receiving reports about Indian troops crossing the international border, the Council met again on 6 September. It adopted a resolution calling upon both sides to take all steps for immediate ceasefire. It asked the Secretary-General to report within three days on the implementation of the resolution.

News of the Indian troops having reached the outskirts of Lahore and of Indian military planes bombing military targets in Pakistan electrified the nation. Suddenly note was being taken of the gravest crises on the subcontinent. Possibility of

China going to Pakistan's help and USA going in aid of India was being discussed in diplomatic circles. There was speculation about the Soviet Union, which had expressed concern about China's expansionist policies. With two Commonwealth countries at war, position of the United Kingdom was getting difficult. Harold Wilson, who had successfully intervened in the Rann of Kutch, sent messages to both Shastri and Ayub, urging immediate ceasefire. He started that: "A most dangerous situation has been created which may have the gravest consequences not only for India and Pakistan but also for peace of the world."

Wilson added that: "Both governments bear responsibility for the steady escalation which has subsequently occurred, and today's attack in Lahore area presents us with a completely new situation."

Wilson's message implied that India was as much to blame for the war on the subcontinent as Pakistan. That puzzled Indian political circles. Shastri, more or less, brushed aside that message. Bias on the part of Britain would rule out the United Kingdom from playing any effective role in events after the ceasefire.

On the other hand, President Johnson, already heavily involved in Vietnam, was working through the Security Council that was then presided over by his UN representative Goldberg. He was very much concerned with possibility of China intervening in the conflict in aid of Pakistan. Following Chinese Vice Prime Minister's visit to Rawalpindi on 4 September, China was looking for an opportunity to demonstrate its friendship with Pakistan.

UN Security Council Resolution of 5 September, at which Foreign Secretary C.S. Jha was present, was satisfactory from India's point of view. The Council had requested the Secretary-General to "exert all possible efforts to give effect to this resolution and to keep the Council promptly informed on the implementation of the resolutions and on the situation in the area."

Between 6 and 10 September, Chavan was fully occupied with conduct of war. The most crucial advance towards Lahore had been stalled on the east bank of Ichhogil canal. Tank battles at Assal Uttar in the Khem Karan Sector were to take place and there was delay in launching attack in the Sialkot Sector. He was pushing the COAS for some spectacular results on the battleground because he was aware of the international pressures to effect a ceasefire.

President Ayub Khan found himself beleaguered and sought help from various countries. His appeal to the USA found no response. Shah of Iran and the president of Turkey wanted to help but their military hardware was from the USA, without whose approval they could not send to Pakistan. China was the only country from whom Pakistan could expect help at that stage. It would come much later on 17 September in a strange way.

In the meantime pursuant to the Security Council resolution of 6 September, U Thant left New York to visit the subcontinent. On 9 September he landed in Rawalpindi and met Foreign Minister Bhutto and President Ayub. On 10 September he continued with his talks. Pakistan was not prepared to agree to a ceasefire. This was the final message with which U Thant left Rawalpindi on the morning of 11 September for New Delhi.

U Thant's Diplomacy

16

On 12 September 1965 Chavan recorded:

U Thant has come today. Meet PM at 4 p.m.

Meeting with PM at 7 p.m. He told details to me and Sardarji (Swaran Singh, the Foreign Minister) of his talks with U Thant.

U Thant briefed the prime minister about discussions in Rawalpindi. Pakistan Government had admitted that its forces had crossed the Indian territory. They also spelt out conditions for ceasefire. Shastri rejected Pakistan's terms straightaway.

Secretary-General wrote to Shastri and Ayub, urging them to suspend fighting. He requested a reply by 7.30 a.m. of 14 September at the latest.

On 13 September Chavan wrote:

EEC at 9 a.m. U Thant's proposals were placed before us. He wants a final reply by 15 (September) morning. We, particularly I and TT (Krishnamachari), pressed for conditional acceptance. But no final view could emerge.

4 p.m. Executive of the Congress party in Parliament daily briefing—very critical of peace proposals.

6.30 p.m. ECC again. General view that emerged was that we should accept the proposal of cessation of hostilities.

But made our position clear on the following two points:

The new pockets occupied in Kashmir should not be given up as they were essential for preventing infiltration; and

Kashmir is no longer a problem of political negotiations as far as India was concerned.

PM's dinner in U Thant's honour was a quiet, peaceful affair.

There was intense fighting in the Sialkot Sector. Pakistan had lost over 50 tanks. Indians had made significant advances in the Haji Pir bulge area and also launched attack, in the far off Barmer Sector of Rajasthan, intended to tie down the Pakistan Division in that area. Chavan was not agreeable to a simple ceasefire at that stage.

It was clear that there were differences within the cabinet. These were reported by Selig S. Harrison in the Washington Post of 14 and 15 September. According to him the ministers were divided over the timing of the truce. General Chaudhuri had urged the ECC to avoid the cessation of hostilities at that point. The army, he said, was on the verge of a decisive victory in the Punjab and should be allowed to inflict maximum damage on Pakistan forces. He was strongly supported by the defence minister. According to Harrison, the prime minister held out for acceptance of the UN resolution.

Because of differences within the ECC, India requested an extension of time. This was accepted by the Secretary-General. He notified the two capitals that the proposed ceasefire was postponed to 6.30 p.m., on 15 September. Obviously, no consensus was reached within the ECC next day, as is evident from Chavan's entry on 14 September. He wrote:

In the noon leaders of the opposition were called by PM and ECC (and) Executive Committee (of the Congress party in Parliament) also endorsed the same.

At 4 p.m. ECC met again. Here PM produced a different draft than the one that was shown yesterday (Chavan has added in Marathi: I did not like this sleight-of-hand). I felt that the draft was too long and vague. I said so. COAS suggested some changes.

There were intensive discussions in the ECC about the pros and cons of the ceasefire. On 14 September the Indian prime minister expressed his willingness for a truce. He wrote to the Secretary-General: "In deference to the wishes of the Security Council and to the appeals which we have received from many friendly countries, we accept your proposal for an immediate ceasefire."

India conveyed its willingness to order a ceasefire effective from 6.30 a.m. on Thursday, 16 September, provided U Thant confirmed by 9 a.m. on 15 September that Pakistan was also agreeable to do so. The prime minister, however, made it clear that such a truce would apply only to uniformed soldiers. India would be free to deploy the army to deal with the thousands of armed infiltrators who had crossed into the State of Jammu and Kashmir. U Thant refused to accept any conditions being attached and replied, "I have no right under the security resolution to give undertakings...".

The ECC considered U Thant's letter and 'decided to reply in a more agreeable way'. Shastri replied the next day and 'reaffirmed willingness to order a simple ceasefire and cessation of hostilities as proposed by you, as soon as you are able to confirm to me that the government of Pakistan has agreed to do so as well.' U Thant accepted Shastri's assurance and forwarded it to Pakistan.

Chavan added on 14 September:

At 5 p.m. I had discussions with U Thant for about 45 minutes in my office. Events since 5 August were recounted and I put across my point of view. Defence Secretary and the COAS were present.

September 15, 1965

ECC to consider the reply to U Thant. It was decided after some discussion to reply in a more agreeable way. But it is strange that U Thant has again equated both India and Pakistan.

Met Executive at 4 p.m., had a usual type of discussion. I gave them some information on the happenings on the front.

ECC meeting again at 5 p.m. U Thant has sent another proposal, offering his own mediation. This proposal surprised even P.M. Does it mean that U Thant expected the failure of the proposal of ceasefire?

The whole affair looked like a mechanical process.

PM authorised the announcement to be broadcast that war efforts will continue unabated.

At 6 p.m. met Chiefs of Staff. Informed them of the results of the ECC and asked them to take a close review of their strategies.

September 16, 1965

No morning meeting today. Went straight to Lok Sabha. PM made a statement on U Thant talks and its results. It was very well received in the house. All the opposition party leaders supported the stand of government. Only Dr. Ram Manohar Lohia, in his own typical way, said: "We are behind the army. We are not behind the government—but on its side.

It was a heartening sight to see all parties united on a major national issue.

President Ayub replied to U Thant on 16 September, several hours after the expiry of the deadline. Several conditions were attached. The Pakistan president said a ceasefire could be 'meaningful' only if followed by steps 'to evolve an effective machinery and procedure that would lead to a final settlement of the Kashmir dispute.' On the morning of 16 September, Shastri informed Parliament that since no reply as stipulated by the Secretary-General had been received from Pakistan, our defence forces would have to continue the operations with unabated vigour.

At that stage, Chavan was eager to end the stalemate in the Sialkot sector. He knew that the ceasefire was imminent. Also, he could not take the Chinese threats lightly.

September 17, 1965

ECC at 9 a.m. at prime minister's house to consider Chinese note. Meeting lasted nearly 2 hours.

It was decided to agree to the joint inspection and send an early reply. But the general feeling was that (the) Chinese would not accept this proposal. It was just an excuse to start trouble for India in support of Pakistan. The main political purpose seems to be to see that Pakistan does not get weak so as to accept ceasefire proposal under the pressure of USA and

Russia. Militarily to see that pressure on Pakistan is relieved and also to give military support to Kashmir LOC (Line of Actual Control).

Prime minister made a statement in Parliament at 3.30 p.m. It was soberly received.

First news of the movement of Chinese Army started coming in.

Tuting in Siang Division of NEFA and Chhamb Valley (Sikkim/Bhutan) were mentioned.

Had a long talk with COAS about Chinese threat and our position in different places.

Prime Minister called in the evening. He was in a mood to talk. We discussed in great length the Chinese threat. The People's Republic of China had been carefully monitoring the outcome of the conflict. On 8 September, when the Pakistani armoured offensive was beginning in Punjab, the Chinese made the first of a series of threats against India. In a formal note, China accused India of violating the Sikkim border on several occasions during July and August. Demanding a halt to further provocations the note warned that "India must bear the responsibility for all the consequences arising therefrom."

On 17 September, at 1 a.m. Peking time, a note was delivered to the Indian Chargé de Affaires. China accused India of maintaining fifty-six military installations on the Tibetan side of the Sikkim-Tibetan border and demanded that, "The Indian Government dismantle all its military works of aggression on the Chinese side..." within two days, or otherwise, "The Indian government must bear full responsibility for all the grave consequences arising therefrom." The Chinese also demanded the return of our Tibetans, 800 sheep and 59 yaks allegedly abducted from Tibet.

After a two-hour meeting of the ECC that morning, the prime minister made a statement in Parliament. Shastri said, "We do hope that China would not take advantage of the present situation and attack India." He added further, "The House may rest assured that if we are attacked, we shall fight for our freedom with grim determination. The might, be it of

China or Pakistan, will not deter us from defending our territorial integrity."

In reply to the Chinese note, Shastri told Parliament that a number of Indian defence structures, built on the Sikkim side of the border in September 1962, had been abandoned in November 1962. He said India would again offer joint inspection of the border.

September 18, 1965

At 11.30 (a.m.) had a two-hour discussion in the prime minister's room in South Block when both Chiefs of Staff (Chief of Army Staff Gen. Chaudhuri and Air Marshal Arjan Singh), the Cabinet Secretary, Home Secretary, Defence Secretary and L.K. Jha were present. General review of our objective was taken. Supply position was considered. Some early decision was necessary in Chhamb Sector. This was necessary (for) both political and military reasons. I stressed this point. COAS will look into this.

This meeting was necessary to clear the minds. USA, USSR and UK were to be approached.

Apparently, the day was devoted to analysing Chinese intentions. Their threat could not be taken lightly. Diplomatic moves had already been initiated to seek help from the UK, the USSR and the USA. At the same time, there was much behind-the-scene activities in the United Nations Security Council. U Thant had returned to New York and the delegates had begun working on a new resolution for peace on the subcontinent.

September 20, 1965

In my meeting with the Chiefs of Staff, I mentioned to them about the possibility of ceasefire as Security Council resolution was expected any time. What was their view?

COAS told me that he had prepared an assessment from (the) military point of view and he would show it to me later.

I think it is good that the military and political thinking was moving in the same direction.

Chinese extended their ultimatum by three days. Very clever people.

ECC (met) in the evening. Security Council Resolution had come by this time ordering ceasefire by the morning of 22nd. ECC generally discussed and adjourned to meet next day.

When I was in the Chiefs of Staff meeting at 6 p.m. message came that I should meet prime minister with defence secretary and chiefs of army staff. L.K. Jha was present. We met at 7 p.m. at prime minister's.

After some preliminary discussion about the military point of view, it was agreed that prime minister should send to U Thant, through G. Parthasarthy (India's Permanent Representative to the UN) (a message) confirming our willingness to order simple ceasefire if Pakistan is agreeable.

The army was on top of the situation and ready to unreservedly support the simple ceasefire. This would also deflect the Chinese threat.

The prime minister, after a high-level review, accepted the proposal and the theatre of operations shifted to the United Nations in New York. The Chinese had watered down their threat by unilaterally announcing the extension of the time limit by 72 hours, on expiration of the original deadline. China thus attempted to extract the last ounce of profit from the situation.

September 21, 1965

This was a fast-moving day. Morning brought the news of China's firing in Nathula (Sikkim) and other places. Three days' extension was just a bluff. Our troops were ordered to reply to the fire, if fired upon and to take defensive positions if a major attack came.

ECC met. Prime minister told them about the message already sent to U Thant. ECC agreed without much discussion.

Party executive met and endorsed prime minister's action with enthusiasm.

All party leaders met. They thought that prime minister's action of sending the message to U Thant a diplomatic and wise move.

News came in the evening that Bhutto (Foreign Minister) left Pakistan on way to New York to address the Security Council.

I think he will bark and bark there and ultimately agree to the ceasefire.

As anticipated, the Chinese threat disappeared in the next twenty-four hours. High level diplomacy and the war of words at the UN had begun. Bhutto, the Foreign Minister of Pakistan, was on his way to New York.

Ceasefire Drama

17

September 22, 1965

I was in bed at 5 a.m. when P.V.R. Rao phoned to tell me that Parthasarthy has phoned to say that (the) Secretary-General wants us to declare unilateral ceasefire. It was an absurd suggestion. I told him it is better that ECC meet to consider. I am dead opposed to such (a) suicidal thing.

8.30 (a.m.) ECC met. I put forward my point of view. ECC agreed. A message was sent to Parthasarthy.

As stated earlier on 20 September, the Security Council had in a unanimous resolution—with Jordan abstaining—demanded a ceasefire on the morning of 22 September. The Council promised to consider 'what steps could be taken to assist towards a settlement of the political problem underlying the conflict. Without mentioning China, the resolution called on all states to refrain from any action that might aggravate the situation in the area. This was a warning to Peking.

While between 8-13 September, U Thant was busy on the subcontinent to bring about a ceasefire, China was carefully monitoring the diplomatic manoeuvres. It was typical of Chinese to make their presence felt by launching a personal attack on U Thant. On 14 September, the *Peoples Daily* of Peking stated that: "The US is behind U Thant's current mission to India and Pakistan and UN Secretary-General is merely acting as Washington's political broker." Apparently they wished to give comfort to President Ayub without in any way committing themselves to any action on the ground.

Shastri's assessment that Chavan shared, was that the Chinese would not mount a major attack as they had done in 1962 because they had no important and immediate objective of their own to achieve. Even the Pakistanis could not expect China to invite wrath of the United States. Both superpowers had in their own way given China unambiguous warning against involvement in the Indo-Pak War. The Chinese had therefore worked out some imaginary grievance on the border, enough to bruise India's morale but not enough to invite US reprisal.

India had accepted the resolution but Pakistan was refusing to do so. At this stage the Secretary-General suggested to India's representative G. Parthasarthy that India considers the declaration of a unilateral ceasefire. Chavan stoutly opposed the proposal. While the ECC was in session, word of Bhutto addressing the Security Council came in. After indulging in last-minute dramatics, at the precise moment when the original UN deadline was to expire at 3 a.m. New York time, he announced that President Ayub had ordered a ceasefire in the interest of international peace.

SECTION III

Preparation for Role 18

Chavan's Diary clearly brings out the role that he played in the conduct of the India-Pakistan War. It was a role for which he had to prepare himself from the day he landed in Delhi on November 20, 1962 to assume the office of the defence minister.

Fortunately, when he arrived to take oath of office the next morning, the Chinese declared unilateral ceasefire. That gave Chavan some time to settle down in his new post, although he was not sure as to when the Chinese would re-launch their attack. Therefore, from the outset, Chavan devoted himself to two tasks: One, to reorganize, rebuild, and resurrect the armed forces of India, especially the army. Secondly, to pull out the army's leadership from their demoralized state and re-establish relationship of trust and confidence between the political and military leadership. How well he performed these two tasks was evident in the 1965 Indo-Pak War.

At political level it was a challenge to re-establish relationship of respect and trust between the political and military leadership. His predecessor, Krishna Menon, had, with his behaviour and style of working, created a rift between the two, that increased during the 1962 India-China War. Chavan was conscious that he had a difficult task on hand because to some extent the prime minister, who had firmly stood by Menon, was also involved in contributing to that rift and was branded as one of the 'guilty men' of the 1962. That made Chavan's task far more delicate as well.

It was no secret that Pandit Nehru was compelled to oust Krishna Menon under pressure of the Parliament and from senior leaders of his own Congress party. He was likewise forced to invite Y.B. Chavan because he could not offer the defence portfolio to any of his senior colleagues in the cabinet. On Krishna Menon's resigning, there was intense canvassing for the post by several leaders. Their unabashed rivalry and ambition to succeed Menon was shocking at a time when the Chinese forces were poised to enter the plains of Assam. Thus, Chavan's choice was a matter of compulsion and expediency. Pandit Nehru detested acting under pressure and he did not want Chavan to think that he had suddenly become an important leader in Delhi. Therefore, as soon as there was a respite from the war on the frontier, he allowed certain senior politicians to administer 'pin-pricks' to the new defence minister. Biju Patnaik, the Chief Minister of Orissa, who had assumed the role of a senior adviser to the prime minister and who had strategically located his office in Delhi in a room adjoining the prime minister's office took a lead in performing that task. As a consequence, within the first six months in office, on two occasions, Chavan was forced to submit to the prime minister his resignation, which were promptly rejected. That was Pandit Nehru's way of showing Chavan that his presence in Delhi was at PM's will.

Chavan, faced with challenges on several fronts, decided to attend to state of the armed forces on priority basis. There was great deal of demoralisation among middle ranking officers which was aggravated by bickering amongst senior officers of the army. In the aftermath of the humiliation suffered by the army, that was not unexpected. Maj. Gen. D.K. Palit, the then Director of Military Operations in his book *War in High Himalayas* has candidly described: "It was the worst of times for the Indian army, a time to hang down our heads in shame. Fortunately for *amour propre*, the community at large was never told the whole truth about the debacle. Government handouts to the press painted the picture of a valiant Indian army stabbed in the back by a supposedly friendly neighbour and then, after offering fierce resistance, overwhelmed by mass

Chinese forces equipped with superior weapons. The shame that *we* felt was self-imposed, but none the less acute for that."

In that situation, Chavan could restore their morale only if he could confidently apply balm to their hurt and hold prospect of better governance in promotions and placements without favouritism as rampantly indulged by his predecessor. He was, however, not sure that he commanded full trust of Pandit Nehru who still thought that Krishna Menon was wrongly accused of interference in professional matters.

Thus for Chavan the main challenge in the first year was to establish relationship of trust between himself and the prime minister. He succeeded in doing so by his deft-handling of the Henderson Brook's Report of Inquiry into NEFA (North East Frontier Agency—present Arunachal Pradesh) reverses. At the same time, he learnt some "lessons", that helped him in the conduct of the 1965 Indo-Pak War. In this context, it would be relevant to refer to the Henderson Brook's Report which remains an extremely closely guarded secret till this date.

During one of the debates, the prime minister had assured the parliament that an inquiry will be held into the debacle. After much deliberation, Chavan proposed an inquiry by committee of two serving army officers rather than a judicial probe or a public inquiry as expected by the Parliament. Further, instead of the defence ministry appointing a committee, he asked the chief of army staff to set up the same. Accordingly, a two-man committee with Lt. General Henderson Brook and Brigadier P.C. Bhagat was formed. Both officers had impeccable record of service. Henderson Brook, an Australian national, had opted to serve the Indian army after partition. Brigadier Prem Bhagat was the first Indian officer to be conferred the Victoria Cross during the Second Word War for bravery on the battlefield. Their report was presented by the COAS to Chavan on 2 July 1963. The report contained a great deal of information of an operational nature, formations and deployment of the Indian Army. In 1963 it was considered too sensitive to be made public and although outdated today the report unfortunately remains secret. Author is the only person alive who had examined the report for preparing the statement that Chavan presented to the Parliament.

During the conduct of the inquiry, Chavan was apprehensive that the committee may cast aspersions on the role of the prime minister or the defence minister. His main worry was to find a way to defend the government and at the same time to ensure that the morale of the armed forces was not further adversely affected. For that he repeatedly emphasized in the Parliament that the inquiry was a fact-finding one and to 'learn lessons' for the future and it was *not* a witch-hunt to identify and punish the officers responsible for the debacle.

It was a tribute to his sagacity and political maturity that he performed his role to full satisfaction of the Parliament and also earned gratitude of the prime minister. Some lessons that he learnt are to be found in the statement that he presented to the Parliament (Reproduced in Annexure). But it is also a fact that while doing so, he also *suppressed* certain critical observations. A few words about those might throw light on Chavan's conduct at political level in the 1965 War.

Contrary to general expectation, the report did not directly indict any political leaders. It was done obliquely. On the lack of proper political direction, the committee quoted British India's first Commander-in-Chief, Field Marshal Robert's dictum: "The art of war teaches us not to rely on the likelihood of the enemy not coming, but on our own readiness to receive him; nor on the chance of not attacking, but rather on the fact that we have made our position unassailable."

There was another observation: "the Higher Direction of War and the actual command set-up of the army were obviously out of touch with reality." In a way, this was an indirect indictment of the political leadership and the manner in which operations in NEFA had been handled. Chavan found these observations as very harsh judgment on Pandit Nehru's handling of India's relations with the Peoples Republic of China and for which many felt at that time that he was so much wedded to the Panchsheel that he refused to believe that

China had some other intentions. By accepting that comment publicly, he did not want to cause any more anguish to the prime minister who was already shattered by the perfidy of the China's leadership in subscribing to the Panchsheel but all the time preparing to attack India. At the same time, he did not want to formally reject that observation, because that might further aggravate the morale of the very same senior officers on whom he depended to get the army into shape to face any future aggression. He decided to *suppress* those observations.

So far as the Parliament was concerned he performed so ably that at the end of the debate, the leader of the opposition profusely thanked him for his candid reply to the debate. That way, politically, Chavan established his own identity. He also earned trust and confidence of the prime minister for the manner in which he handled the most severe indictment that Pandit Nehru had to face in his long parliamentary career.

The report was a great education for the novice defence minister. He made copious notes in red ink to help him understand the military jargon. Those 'two observations' would offer guidelines to Chavan to shape his own role as a defence minister. He also earned kudos of his service chiefs for not carrying out 'witch hunt'. His relation of mutual trust and respect to each one of them was crucial to conduct of 1965 War as evident from the Diary and that is elaborated in the next chapter.

Defence Minister and the Chiefs

19

Over a period of three years between 1962-65, what Chavan had accomplished for the three services, can be briefly described in the history of India's defence services as one of expansion, reformation, restructuring and of revitalization. He undertook these tasks immediately on assuming office. During the period, the size of the army was expanded and it was equipped with modern weapons. Through Short Service Commissions, large scale recruitment was undertaken. New facilities were set up to train for mountain warfare and specially equipped for the task. At the same time, expansion and modernization of the Air Force was undertaken. A number of production factories were set up for manufacture of arms, equipment and ammunition. Plans were laid for expansion and acquisition of ships for the Indian Navy and to undertake indigenous production. All this was achieved in his systematic working style and by his considerable administrative skills. But his main achievement was to establish close rapport and relationship of trust with the service chiefs that had been deeply affected because of Krishna Menon's style of man management.

Chavan's achievement is evident from his Diary of 1965 Indo-Pak War that throws light on the relationship between the chief of army staff, the chief of air staff and Y.B. Chavan and how they worked as a close team. During the war, Chavan often acted as a friend, guide and sometime as a nurse to the COAS and the CAS.

Chavan and Gen. J.N. Chaudhuri

Background of two was as diverse as could be. Chavan, born in a poor family, had a modest education. His earthy rural personality was a contrast to Chaudhuri's swagger and affluent bearing. He was generally known in the defence circles as a man with large size ego. When India became independent, he was one of the few Indian officers who had risen to the rank of a brigadier in the Indian Army. As a Major General, he commanded Indian troops in undertaking military operation for Hyderabad State and was appointed Military Governor of Hyderabad. Later, he also commanded operations for liberation of Goa. After holding several appointments, he was posted to Poona as Southern Area Commander where in October 1962, he had been informed that he would soon stand retired from the army. Unexpectedly, on 19 November 1962, he was asked to come over to Delhi to succeed Gen. P.N. Thapar, the COAS, who had resigned taking responsibility for the debacle of the Indian Army.

On 21 November 1962, Y.B. Chavan flew to Delhi in the evening by Indian Airlines flight. On landing, he was greeted at the bottom of the stairway by Chaudhuri who introduced himself as the newly appointed *acting* chief of army staff. That came as a complete surprise to Chavan and he felt a little peeved that the prime minister had not even informed him about the appointment. Wisely, he kept his feelings to himself. On taking over the office of the defence minister, Chavan sensed that the previous day's upheaval had created disquiet in the army headquarters, because several senior officers who were expecting to eventually succeed Gen. Thapar, were unhappy on the appointment of Lt. Gen. Chaudhuri, who was not a popular officer. Chavan, who had had an opportunity of getting to know Chaudhuri when he was at Poona was not overawed with his background. On the other hand, with his acute administrative sense, he felt that in the situation of defeat and despair in which the army leadership was placed, he must help Chaudhuri, who was appointed as *acting* chief with rank of Lt. General, to get firmly on the saddle and for that to let everyone, including all staff officers at the army headquarters to know that the chief had full support of the defence minister. Chaudhuri, in turn, appreciated that attitude since it would help him to project his leadership. With his ability to present ideas in a clear, precise and well-structured language, he was respected in the defence ministry as an 'educated general.' In fact, he was so good on paper that Chavan often wondered how good he would be in warfare!

Chavan's predecessor Krishna Menon had a poor opinion of Gen. Chaudhuri and on a couple of occasions, he volunteered to advise Chavan not to rely too much on Chaudhuri's advice because he was not a general who would ever fight. Chavan was not too much impressed by Krishna Menon's assessment of officers and had decided not to be influenced. He had his own way of judging abilities of officials working under him. He also knew how to inspire and extract the best out of an individual. That is how he handled Gen. Chaudhuri from the outset. How well their relationship developed is evident from a letter that the COAS wrote to the defence minister on completion of one year. On 20 November 1963, Gen. Chaudhuri wrote:

> Exactly a year has passed since I took over as COAS and I well remember your heartening words to me when I met you on your arrival at PALAM, also a year ago this evening.
>
> What has been achieved, and perhaps more important what still remains to be done, in building up the army is best judged by you. However, I can assure you with all sincerity that the greatest single factor which has helped me in carrying out my task has been your unstinted support and trust. I am indeed grateful and this purely personal letter is, if you will accept it, one method of expressing this gratitude.
>
> The future will have its share of fears and frustrations but it will also have its share of joys and triumphs. I can assure you that the army will continue to give its best to you and through you, to the country. I am also sure that as long as I deserve it, your confidence and understanding will remain my greatest support.

True test of their co-operative leadership to the armed forces was to take place during the 1965 Indo-Pak War. That is evident from several entries in the Diary.

On 2 September Chavan wrote: *COAS came to unburden his mind, looked somewhat depressed.*

Next day he recorded: *COAS came in the evening. He was in good mood. He said he was sorry that he was somewhat depressed yesterday. I can understand this. He has to open his mind; pour it out somewhere. It is good he is doing with me.*

On 4 September he wrote: *Gave me the resume of the events in Chhamb last night and today. He was rather depressed. Discussed with him plans of the next move fixed for tomorrow.*

Later, on several occasions when he found that Chaudhuri was unsure of himself, he asked him to visit the Front and get first-hand assessment of the situation. Those visits proved useful for Gen. Chaudhuri, although on two such visits, he had acrimonious and heated exchanges with Lt. Gen. Harbaksh Singh, the Western Area Army Commander. However, all this helped him to assess situation in the correct perspective and not run the operations seated in the south block. At the end of the war, Chavan gave all credit to the COAS and to the chief of air staff for the success.

On 22 September, after the Emergency Cabinet Committee (ECC) meeting, Chavan wrote:

Cabinet colleagues warmly congratulated me.

Army and air force have become now for us the symbols of our national pride and glory. A great day for me. A great day for Chaudhuri and Arjan Singh.

It was just then (that I) remembered a talk with Krishna Menon only a week ago. He told me that I depended too much on Chaudhuri and he is a general who will never fight. I told him that I disagreed with him. He was going by his personal dislikes. I have told him that from what I have seen of him (Chaudhuri) in the last 3 years, I am sure if it comes to vindicate the honour of (the) Indian army, Chaudhuri will fight. And today, I was vindicated in my judgment of the man. He fought and fought well.

It is, however, to be noted that while the Parliament and the political leadership may have appreciated Gen. Chaudhuri's leadership, many knowledgeable defence analysts were critical of his role in directing the operations. His inaction in not pressing attack across the Punjab border was widely criticised. According to them, the Pakistanis exploited India's surrender of the initiative by mounting their own grand offensive. Thus, there was not much gain in terms of territory. Likewise in operations except capture of the Haji Pir Pass and the high performance of a brigade of tanks in the Khem Karan area, there was not much to show as gains. Pakistan claimed a stalemate and many agreed with that view.

There is no doubt that at one stage Chaudhuri had been hit by panic from the shock of the near disaster at Khem Karan. On receiving unnecessarily alarmist report from XI Corps Commander, he rushed from Delhi to Harbaksh Singh's HQ in the Punjab and ordered him to abandon the Amritsar salient and pulled back behind the Beas. Harbaksh Singh rightly asked to give tactical order in writing. The crisis passed next day when the out-gunned Centurions and Shermans of the Second Independent Armoured Brigade and the guns of 4 Mountain Division played havoc with the Patton tanks of Pakistan's Armoured Division in one of the great tactical victories of the war.

According to some, it was Chaudhuri's misreading of dynamic of battle logistics that caused the crowning blunder of the war. At the commencement of the hostilities, the forward movement of material from Central Ordnance Depots was set in automatic motion without regard to the fact that their requirement would clearly vary from sector- to-sector and must be assessed according to the intensity and the strain of fighting. As a result, sectors in the thick of fighting were running short of ammunition. While large dumps of unused ammunition were lying in sectors where the fighting had not been intensive. That is how on 20 September when the prime minister asked Chaudhuri whether India could expect to gain if the war continued for a few days more, Chaudhuri informed PM that the army was coming to an end of its ammunition holdings and could not sustain the fighting for much longer. Chaudhuri advised acceptance of ceasefire proposal. It was later discovered that in overall terms only 14-20 per cent of the Indian army's ammunition stock had been used up. According to critics, at the moment of our greatest advantage, the army chief's non-comprehension of the intricacies of the long-range logistics deprived India of a decisive victory.

Gen. Chaudhuri was also criticized after the war for showing lack of daring. Well-known senior journalist and former Editor of the *Hindustan Times*, late Durga Das, in his memoirs from 'Curzon to Nehru' wrote critically about Chaudhuri. Durga Das wrote:

> Chaudhuri is reckoned in many quarters to have betrayed a measure of hesitancy in the conduct of the hostilities, if not lack of military daring. Indeed, members of the Cabinet's Emergency Committee felt that Chaudhuri had to be egged on to fight. There is an impression that he erred in not marching our armed forces into Sialkot when it was known that all communications from the Pakistan side with this vital stronghold had been cut, and it was believed that the enemy had pulled out of the city. The failure to occupy Sialkot was significant against the background of pronouncements at the highest level.

Several others asked the same question: Why did the Indian Army fail to take Lahore or Sialkot when these prizes were within its grasp? In Parliament, there was an impression created by Lal Bahadur Shastri and Chavan's statements to believe that Lahore and Sialkot would be taken. According to Durga Das, when asked to take action, Chaudhuri told Shastri that "We must move with the caution and wisdom of an elephant. We will take them in God's good time."

When the author discussed this matter with Chavan, he explained that after the fiasco on the Ichhogil canal, any idea to capture Lahore had to be given up. Also, by that time it was realised that it would not be wise to tie down a large part of the Indian Army inside any city when the Chinese had already started belligerent moves in the Northeast. Perhaps, it was a wise decision because at the end of the war, the situation on the ground was a kind of stalemate with a slight edge in favour of India. Battles inside the cities would have caused large-scale deaths and destruction of property and led to bitterness in minds of civilian population of Pakistan.

It may be easy to target Gen. Chaudhuri's lack of daring because at the end of the conflict except for the capture of the Haji Pir Pass and high performance of a brigade of tanks in the Khem Karan Sector there was not much to show as gains. Pakistan claimed a stalemate and many agreed with that view. Nonetheless, in fairness to the COAS Gen. J.N. Chaudhuri, several give credit to him for restoring in good measure the public image of the Army which had plummeted during the 1962 Indo-China War.

Chavan and Air Marshal Arjan Singh

When Chavan became the defence minister, Air Marshal A.M. Engineer, popularly known as Apsy Engineer, was the Chief of the Indian Air Force. Air Vice Marshal Arjan Singh was the Deputy Chief of Air Staff. A tall, handsome Sikh, and with an athletic build, he looked very impressive in Air Force blue uniform. Always polite and soft-spoken, with prematurely greying beard, he looked much older than his age. Over a period, Arjan Singh had greatly impressed Chavan. Contrary to sagely looks and contemplative nature, Chavan found him full of dash and daring when occasion demanded. This is evident from several entries in the War Diary.

On 1 September, Arjan Singh, without a moment's hesitation on a request from the COAS, agreed to undertake bombing mission to halt Pakistani armoured thrust in the Chhamb Sector. While doing so he did not fail to warn the defence minister that in the fading light and with combat at a close quarter, it was difficult for the Air Force to distinguish friend and foe and some casualties on the Indian side were expected. That was the correct assessment and Chavan was glad that he could inform the Emergency Cabinet Committee in advance about it. Otherwise, the IAF would have invited uncalled criticism from his own cabinet colleagues.

The Diary shows that as operations became wider in scope, Chavan found Air Marshal Arjan Singh showing great mental balance and serenity even when the Indian Air Force had suffered great losses. At the same time, progressively, Arjan Singh got enthused with the operations and on occasions, Chavan had to restrain him.

On 7 September, he wrote:

Bombing by both sides in East Pakistan has created a problem. I told CAS to hold his hand in East Pakistan. We do not want any wasteful escalation there. Politically also, it would be unwise to do anything which might provoke China at this moment. He (CAS) agreed.

Later on 14 September, Chavan wrote:

Reports of Pak attacks on Barrackpore and Agartala came. CAS was keen that we give him permission to start things in East Pakistan'. I had told him to wait for a day. One more incident and he is free to go ahead.

On 12 September, when Chavan gave permission to bomb Sargodha Air Force base near Peshawar, in retaliation of the Pakistan Air Force attacking on Kulaikunda base in West Bengal, Chavan recorded:

When he (Air Marshal Arjan Singh) is asked to go ahead on a new task CAS even walks as a dancing bird. A real fighting Sikh! And yet how soft and gentle.

At the end of the conflict, on 22 September, when the prime minister personally congratulated the COAS and CAS, Chavan wrote:

Air Marshal Arjan Singh is a jewel of a person; quietly efficient and fine; unexcitable but a very able leader.

After the war, the post of the chief of air staff was upgraded to that of air chief marshal. On 20 January 1966 Arjan Singh wrote to Y.B. Chavan:

> I am writing this to thank you sincerely for upgrading the appointment of the CAS and for promoting me to the rank of Air Chief Marshal. It is indeed a great honour to the Indian Air Force and myself. I would like to express my deep gratitude for your kindness to me at all times.

> I shall never forget your words "Do not worry about the past, the future is more important", said to me after I reported to you the serious mishap at Pathankot on the 6th September 1965.* Your coolness in adversity and capacity to take bold decisions was a great inspiration to me throughout the conflict.

Years later after he retired as the chief of air staff and served the country as India's envoy in Nairobi and Berne. Much later he also served as the Lt. Governor of Delhi. He remains the same gentle person.

Chavan and Vice-Admiral D.S. Soman

In November 1962, with all the spotlight on the Army and the Air Force, the Navy had been relegated to background. The Naval Chief, Vice-Admiral D.S. Soman, who hailed from Poona, Maharashtra, felt left out from all the attention that the other two services were receiving because of the nature of the threat facing the country. In Rear Admiral S.M.S. Nanda, he had a very able Deputy Chief. He would later succeed Soman.

In his War Diary, Chavan mentions CNS on two occasions.

On 11 September, Chavan wrote: *Had discussions in the presence of the PM with CNS (Admiral S.M.S. Nanda). Necessay orders were given.*

Three days later, on 14 September, he wrote: *Had a talk with CNS about his plans. He is rather too keen to do something. I had to restrain him.*

Between these two entries lies a story. The main theatre of war was the Punjab and Jammu and Kashmir. No one gave much thought or considered an active role for the Indian

---

*On 6 September Pakistan Air Force attacked Kulaikunda base in West Bengal. They also dropped paratroops between Guahati and Shillong in Assam. Chavan did not want any escalation in the east and had advised CAS not to initiate any action on that side. However, due to some misunderstanding, the same day Canberras of the Eastern Air Command attacked Chittagong and Dacca airfields. In retaliation Pakistan Air Force attacked Indian bases at Bagdogra, Calcutta and Kulaikunda, hitting a number of aircraft on the ground.

Navy. In fact, soon after the operations started, the defence ministry had given written instructions that the Indian Navy was not to proceed more than 200 miles beyond Bombay nor North of the parallel of Porbandar. Apparently, India did not wish to extend the war to the seas as the Navy was still to be re-equipped with naval equipment negotiated with the Soviet Union. It was feared that especially on the Eastern board which was generally unprotected, Pakistan Navy may carry out widescale attacks. India was ill-equipped to face such an eventuality and therefore did not wish to provoke Pakistan.

However, when the Pakistan Army faced difficult situation, perhaps as a diversionary tactic, on 10 September the main task force of the Pakistan Navy, including the cruiser Babur, sneaked out of Karachi in the dead of night and made its way to Dwarka, at the tip of Saurashtra and entrance to the Gulf of Kutch, which it proceeded to bombard. The Pakistani naval raid at Dwarka left the officers and men of the Indian Navy infuriated and greatly humiliated.

This incident naturally upset the naval chief and his deputy. Nonetheless, considering the overall battle situation, and the international pressure that was being exerted through the United Nations, both Shastri and Chavan agreed not to allow the Navy to undertake any offensive or retaliatory task.

Admiral Kohli, who was in 1965 Deputy Chief of Naval Staff (later to become the chief), in his book *We Dared*, has described his talk with Admiral Soman on the subject. In Prologue, he writes: Admiral Soman, on being asked by me recently, gave his version of what had transpired in his characteristic forthright manner. Here it is in his own words:

> As far as I remember, it was the morning after the evening of the start of the war that I got a file from the ministry signed by Sarin who was then joint secretary, saying that the Navy is not to initiate any offensive action against Pakistan at sea and is not to operate above the latitude of Probandar except in pursuit of any Pak Navy offensive action. I immediately contacted the Minister, Mr. Y.B. Chavan, and asked to see him; at our meeting I

> strongly protested against this order and said in any case I cannot accept it from a joint secretary in the ministry. If I remember correctly, Mr. Chavan initialled the directive and asked me if that would do. I replied that in that case I would like to see the prime minister.
>
> Arrangements were made for me to see the Prime Minister Shastriji, next morning, and I had about twenty minutes with him. On his assurance that it was a cabinet decision—I am not sure whether he too initialled the file—I accepted it on the understanding that should I consider it necessary, I may be allowed to see the President of India as the Commander-in-Chief.

According to Navy brass, it was natural of them to expect playing offensive role and attack the Pak fleet in their base as well as the port of Karachi. But as clearly spelt out in the directive to the chiefs, the prime minister and the defence minister had decided to limit the hostilities. At the end of hostilities Y.B. Chavan wrote to the CNS:

> I greatly appreciated the silent but effective role that the navy played in defence of the country. The navy protected islands which were vital to our security, guard our ports and the long Indian coastline. All merchant ships destined for our ports reached safely and our international trade was not permitted to be interfered with by the Pakistan Navy. I take this opportunity to emphasise again that the Navy has done and achieved all that the government desired of it within the bounds and compass allotted to it.

That was his way to sooth bruised ego of the naval brass. The Navy got an opportunity to play a significant role in the 1971 Indo-Pakistan War.

Higher Direction of War 20

Role of a Defence Minister

Chavan knew that he could provide 'Higher Direction of War' as expected of him, only through the chiefs, and not by disrupting the chain of command, as his predecessor had done. That meant working closely with the chiefs. For that he devised a mechanism of daily morning meetings. Along with the three chiefs, the defence secretary, the foreign secretary and the director of intelligence also attended. These meetings, soon to be labelled as "prayer-meetings", were an efficient clearing-house to exchange information, to share assessments and plans, to hasten decision-making and to bring about close co-ordination and also help to bring about greater understanding amongst principal policy makers and the Services, who were responsible for operations in case of war.

As pointed out earlier, the Henderson Brook's Report had obliquely criticized the government at the highest level for absence of the 'Higher Direction of War'. Lt. Gen. B.M. Kaul, the high profile officer who was suddenly projected as commander of the task force and his band of admirers, put all the blame on Krishna Menon and on Pandit Nehru. In his Statement on Inquiry into NEFA reverses, Chavan had cleverly side-stepped the issue by merely stating that:

> That brings me to the next point which is called the higher direction of operations. Even the largest and the best equipped of armies need to be given proper policy guidance and major directives by the government whose instrument it is. These must bear a reasonable relation to the size of the Army and state of its equipment from time to time. An

increase in the size or improving the equipment of the Army costs not only money but also needs time.

With that background in view, as soon as Pakistan had begun operations in the Rann of Kutch in April 1965, the Government made an assessment of Pakistan's intentions and regarded Pakistan's manoeuvres in Kutch as only a smokescreen for her pre-planned intrusions in Kashmir. This assessment guided Gen. J.N. Chaudhuri to prepare for movement and deployment of troops in the North and also start working on the "Operation Riddle".

The Prime Minister Shastri clearly spelt out Government of India's thinking when in his statement before the Lok Sabha on April 28, he said,' "If Pakistan continues to discard reason and persists in its aggressive activities, our Army will defend the country, and it will decide its own strategy and the employment of its manpower and equipment in the manner which seems best." That statement constituted a public directive to the armed forces. Soon after beginning of the hostilities, on 3 September, the defence minister along with his army and air force chiefs had a long meeting with the prime minister to define the country's war aims. These were as follows:

(1) To defend against Pakistan's attempts to grab Kashmir by force and to make it abundantly clear that Pakistan would never be allowed to wrest Kashmir from India.

(2) To destroy the offensive power of Pakistan's armed forces.

(3) To occupy only the minimum Pakistan territory necessary to achieve these purposes which would be vacated after the satisfactory conclusion of the war.

These directions constituted what is called the 'Higher Direction of War' and would enable the army and the air force to plan their offensive operations within the framework of the government's aims and objectives. The War Diary shows how the defence minister guided the army and the air force chiefs to that end. Thus, the political leadership and the military leadership worked as one team and it would appear that to some extent the lessons of the 1962 debacle had been well learnt.

President Ayub greeting PM Lal Bahadur Shastri

Tashkent Conference in session

PM Lal Bahadur Shastri with President Ayub, Kosygin and others

PM Lal Bahadur Shastri signing the Agreement with Y.B. Chavan by his side

A Futile War

21

According to some the conflict of 1965 was waiting to happen. Both India and Pakistan were suffering from a sense of insecurity.

Ceasefire had become effective from 23 September 1965. It was generally conceded that India had effectively defeated Pakistani Army on the battlefields. Large areas of Pakistan were occupied or under control of India's Army. Continued presence of Indian troops on the east side of Ichhogil canal, facing Lahore city was hurting Pakistan's pride. Even in that situation, ground commanders of Pakistani forces had continued efforts to surreptitiously occupy areas near the border and to fire intermittently across the border. Taking into account that situation, the Security Council strongly urged on 27 September to effectively enforce the ceasefire.

Politically, Lal Bahadur Shastri was on the top and his popularity had soared. India perceived him as a new leader after Nehru's death who had defeated Pakistan; not buckled under China's threat and steered India in war and diplomacy. International community was also looking to him to resolve basic issues underlying the war. It was known that only the United States and the USSR could play any role as the United Kingdom had been perceived as partial to Pakistan. Both countries were looking to dialogue to search for enduring peace.

During the conflict, the Prime Minister of USSR, Kosygin, had communicated his willingness to help further process of understanding between the two countries, if acceptable to both. On 23 September 1965, Lal Bahadur Shastri had informed the Parliament of that, and shown readiness to respond positively. On 18 November Zulfikar Ali Bhutto, Foreign Minister of Pakistan also conveyed their willingness. On 3 January 1966, Lal Bahadur Shastri and President Ayub Khan arrived in Tashkent, where Kosygin personally played host to their meeting.

During the discussions over next six days, Kosygin acted as a go-between the two leaders. He made it clear that there could be no reopening of the decision by the Security Council that both countries should withdraw their forces to position as obtaining on 5 August 1965. That meant that India would surrender several key areas conquered by valour and courage, and after much bloodshed. It would require India to give up the Haji Pir Pass, the main ingress route for Pakistani guerrillas into the Valley. After much discussion and strong pressures exerted by the Prime Minister Kosygin, Lal Bahadur Shastri agreed to vacate areas occupied after 5 August 1965. President Ayub on his part had to give up any mention about the future of J&K. That paved the way to the Tashkent Agreement.

Lal Bahadur Shastri's death on 10 January 1966 in Tashkent overshadowed the Tashkent Agreement. Unfortunately, India had lost there what India had gained on the battlefield after shedding so much blood. Nonetheless, it cannot be said that India had fought the war in vain. India's war objectives set by the prime minister and the defence minister in their meeting with the COAS and CAS on 3 September 1965 were largely met.

According to the official historians, although in military terms the contest was a draw, it should be noted that in the overall context it was clear victory for India. The Indian war aim was to preserve the status quo in Jammu and Kashmir and to foil Pakistani attempt to grab it. These limited and defensive aims were fully achieved. India deliberately opted for as short and as limited a conflict as possible. East Pakistan (now Bangladesh) was not attacked. The Indian Navy was held back from any offensive action. Even the IAF was not thrown into battle against Pakistan territory till after the PAF had attacked Indian air bases on the evening of 6 September, causing serious loss at Pathankot. At last ceasefire was accepted when India was still capable of continuing the fight, and when the enemy was showing signs of total exhaustion. So the aggressor was let off lightly. Pakistan would have suffered a crushing defeat if the IAF had launched a full scale pre-emptive attack against the PAF on the morning of 6 September itself, and if the Army had really gone for a kill when the enemy was tottering after 20 September. The Indians, they say, lack, 'the killer instinct', whether it be a battleground or the playfield. In any case, the Indian Government and military leadership accepted a stalemate and refrained from humbling Pakistan, in the belief that this moderation would lead to less bitterness and more friendly relations. But in 1965, as again in 1971, these humane sentiments and noble assessments proved definitely inapplicable in the case of Pakistan. One wonders whether the correct deductions have been made in the quarters concerned.

The status of J&K and the CFL remained unsettled and a source of future trouble. It had been a war to no purpose. India could claim to have defeated Pak designs on Kashmir while Pakistani boasted about halting an invasion of Pakistan by a larger Indian Army. Both sides were content to claim victory to their people.

Was it indeed a futile war?

Future of India-Pakistan Relations: Chavan's Reflections

22

Y.B. Chavan had come to Delhi when the Chinese troops were poised to enter the plains of Assam. During past three years in Delhi he had seen and participated in most important policy issues in the field of defence as well as in the foreign affairs. He had traveled to UK, the USSR and the USA. He had met leaders in these countries and formed his own perceptions of international affairs and the working of the United Nations. With that background, at the end of war, he made in his own hand certain observations that sum up in a distilled form his understanding of what had been achieved and how he saw the future. He wrote:

> *So the first round is over—where is the second round and when?*
>
> *I have a feeling that this is the real beginning of trouble in this part of the world. How we utilize the respite that we are getting is going to decide the future of the country. The dangerous process of encirclement of India by hostile countries is complete. The leading powers of UNO including USSR are not with us on (the) Kashmir issue. We are tragically alone.*
>
> *This is the achievement of our foreign policy—The issue (Kashmir) is basically political. Its solution will have to be political.*
>
> *We have, with good luck, come out of it (the conflict) well. But if we try to make it again purely military, it will be a disastrous mistake. Unless we make quick and radically new moves to break the political isolation that we find ourselves in.*

These reflections are Y.B. Chavan's legacy to our leadership, who are in search of solution to the basic problem that has plagued relations between two neighbours who, not long ago, were one country and whose people wish to live and prosper together. Finally, Chavan added:

> *The ball is now in the political court again—where it should be—and not the military one.*
>
> *I hope we have the vision and courage to accept this challenge to (our) political leadership.*

Annexure

Statement by the Defence Minister Regarding the NEFA Enquiry

September 2, 1963

The Defence Minister, Shri Y.B. Chavan, made the following statement in the Lok Sabha today:

1. Sir, I wish to inform the House of the results of the enquiry to investigate our reverses in the operations occasioned by the Chinese aggression across our northern borders during the months of October-November 1962.

2. Though the officers appointed to enquire into these reverses were asked to examine the operations with particular reference to the Kameng Division of NEFA, they quite rightly came to the conclusion that the developments in NEFA were closely co-related to those in Ladakh and their study of NEFA operations, had to be carried out in conjunction with developments and operations in the Ladakh sector. Thus, the enquiry made and the conclusions emerging from it are results of study into the entire operations on our northern borders.

3. As I had informed the House on 1 April, in reply to a question in the Lok Sabha, with my approval the Chief of Army Staff had ordered a thorough investigation to be carried out to find as to what was wrong with:

(i) our training;

(ii) our equipment;

(iii) our system of command;

(iv) the physical fitness of our troops; and

(v) the capacity of our Commanders at all levels to influence the men under them.

4. While conveying to the House the terms of reference of this enquiry, I had made it clear that the underlying idea in holding this enquiry is to derive military lessons. It was meant to bring out clearly what were the mistakes or deficiencies in the past, so as to ensure that in future such mistakes are not repeated and such deficiencies are quickly made up. Consequently, the enquiring officers had to study in great and intimate detail the extent of our preparedness at the time, the planning and strategic concepts behind it and the way those plans were adjusted in the course of operations. This also necessitated the examination of the developments and events prior to hostilities as also the plans, posture and the strength of the Army at the outbreak of hostility. In the course of the enquiry a very detailed review of the actual operations in both the sectors had to be carried out with reference to terrain, strategy, tactics and deployment of our troops.

5. The conclusions drawn at the end of the report flow from an examination of all these matters in great detail. In these circumstances, I am sure, the House would appreciate that by the very nature of the contents it would not be in the public interest to lay the report on the table of the House. Nor is it possible to attempt even an abridged or edited version of it, consistent with the consideration of security that would not give an unbalanced or incomplete picture to you.

6. I have given deep thought to this matter and it is with great regret that I have to withhold this document from this august House. The publication of this report which contains information about the strength and development of our Forces and their locations would be of invaluable use to our enemies. It would not only endanger our security but affect the morale of those entrusted with safeguarding the security of our borders.

Main Conclusions

7. Before I turn to the main conclusions of this enquiry may I bring to the notice of the House, that I had already

made clear, that this enquiry is the type of enquiry which the Prime Minister had in mind when he promised such an enquiry to the House in November 1962 into the state of military unpreparedness to meet the Chinese invasion. I would like to assure the House that we had at the outset made it clear to those who were entrusted with this enquiry, and they in turn made it clear to the persons whom they found necessary to examine, that our main intention was to derive lessons to help in our future preparedness and not in any way to undertake a witch-hunt into the culpabilities of those who were concerned with or took part in these operations. This was absolutely essential to get a full factual picture of the situation as it obtained in October-November 1962. I may specially mention this to remind the House that in considering these matters, we should never miss the proper sense of perspective or say or do things which could only give heart to the enemy and demoralise our own men. I have no doubt that the House would wish to ensure this spirit to be maintained.

8. The enquiring officers submitted their report to the Chief of Army Staff on 12 May 1963. After obtaining some complementary information the Chief of Army Staff submitted this report along with his comments to me on 2 July. Considering the enormous mass of details that had to be gone into with meticulous care by the enquiring officers, as I have myself seen, I would consider that the report has been completed with commendable speed.

Training of Jawans

9. The first question in the terms of reference was whether our training was found wanting.

The enquiry has revealed that our basic training was sound and soldiers adapted themselves to the mountains adequately. It is admitted that the training of our troops did not have orientation towards operations vis-à-vis the particular terrain in which the troops had to operate. Our training of the troops did not have a slant for a war being launched by China. Thus our troops had no requisite knowledge of the Chinese tactics, and ways of war weapons, equipment and capabilities.

Knowledge of the enemy helps to build up confidence and morale, so essential to the Jawan on the front.

10. The enquiry has revealed that there is certainly need for toughening and battle inoculation. It is, therefore, essential that battle schools are opened at training centres and formations, so that gradual toughening of the battle inoculation can be carried out.

11. It has also revealed that the main aspect of training as well as the higher Commanders' concept of mountain warfare requires to be put right.

12. Training alone, however, without correct leadership will pay little dividends. Thus the need of the moment, above all else, is training in leadership.

Shortage of Equipment

13. The second question was about our equipment. The enquiry has confirmed that there was indeed an overall shortage of equipment both for training and during operations. But it was not always the case that particular equipment was not available at all with the Armed Forces anywhere in the country. The crucial difficulty in many cases was that, while the equipment could be reached to the last point in the plains or even beyond it, it was another matter to reach it in time, mostly by air or by animal or by human transport to the forward formations, who took the brunt of the fighting. This position of logistics was aggravated by two factors:

(i) the fast rate at which troops had to be inducted, mostly from plains to high mountain areas; and the

(ii) lack of properly built roads and other means of communication.

14. This situation was aggravated and made worse because of overall shortage as far as vehicles were concerned and as our fleet was too old and its efficiency not adequate for operating on steep gradients and mountain terrain.

15. Thus, in brief, though the enquiry revealed overall shortage of equipment, it has also revealed that our weapons were adequate to fight the Chinese and compared favourably

with theirs. The automatic rifle would have helped in the cold climate and is being introduced. The enquiry has pinpointed the need to make up deficiency in equipment, particularly suited for mountain warfare, but more so to provide means and modes of communication to make it available to the troops at the right place at the right time. Work on these lines has already been taken in hand and is progressing vigorously.

System of Command

16. The third question is regarding our system of command within the Armed Forces. The enquiry has revealed that there is basically nothing wrong with the system and chain of command, provided it is exercised in an accepted manner at various levels. There is, however, need for realisation of responsibilities at various levels, which must work with trust and confidence in each other. It is also revealed that during the operations, difficulties arose only when there was a departure from the accepted chain of command. There again, such departure occurred mainly due to haste and lack of adequate prior planning.

17. The enquiry has also revealed the practice that crept in the higher Army formations of interfering in tactical details even in the extent of detailing troops for specified tasks. It is the duty of Commanders in the field to make on-the-spot decisions, when so required, and details of operations ought to have been left to them.

Physical Fitness of Troops

18. The fourth question is of the physical fitness of our troops. It is axiomatic that an unacclimatised army cannot be as fit as one which is. The enquiry has revealed that, despite this, our troops both officers and men, stood the rigours of the climate, although most of them were rushed at short notice from the plains. Thus in brief, troops were physically fit in every way from their normal tasks, but they were not acclimatised to fight at the heights at which some of them were asked to make a stand. Where acclimatisation had taken place, such as in Ladakh, the height factor presented no difficulty. Among some middle-age-group officers, there had

been deterioration in standards of physical fitness. This is a matter which is being rectified. The physical fitness among junior officers was good and is now even better.

Capacity of Commanders

19. The fifth point in the terms of reference was about the capacity of the Commanders at all levels during these operations to influence the men under their command. By and large, it had been found that the general standard among the junior officers was fair. At unit level there were good and mediocre Commanding Officers. The proportion of good Commanding Officers and not-so-good was perhaps the same as obtained in any army in the last World War. At Brigade level, but for the odd exception, Commanders were able to adequately exercise their command. It was at higher levels that shortcomings became more apparent. It was also revealed that some of the higher Commanders did not depend enough on the initiative of the lower Commanders, who alone could have the requisite knowledge of the terrain and local conditions of troops under them.

Other Aspects Examined

20. Apart from these terms of reference, the enquiry went into some other important aspects pertaining to the operations, and I would like to inform the House about this also. This relates to the following aspects:

(i) our intelligence;

(ii) our Staff Work and Procedures; and

(iii) our "Higher Direction of Operations".

21. As regards our system and organisation of intelligence, it would obviously not be proper for me to disclose any details. However, it is known that in the Army Headquarters, there is a Directorate of Intelligence under an officer designated as Director of Military Intelligence, briefly known as DMI.

22. The enquiry has brought out that the collection of intelligence in general was not satisfactory. The acquisition of intelligence was slow and the reporting of it vague.

23. Second important aspect of intelligence is its collection and evaluation. Admittedly, because of the vague nature of intelligence, evaluation may not have been accurate. Thus a clear picture of the Chinese build-up was not made available. No attempt was made to link up the new enemy build-up with the old deployment. Thus field formations had little guidance whether there were fresh troops or old ones moving to new locations.

24. The third aspect is dissemination of intelligence. It has come out that much faster means must be employed to send out processed and important information to field formations, if it is to be of any use.

25. There is no doubt that a major overhauling of the intelligence system is required. A great deal has been done during the last six months. The overhauling of the intelligence system is a complex and lengthy task and, in view of its vital importance, I am paying personal attention to this.

Staff Work and Procedures

26. Now about our staff work and procedures. There are clear procedures of staff work laid down at all levels. The enquiry has however revealed that much more attention will have to be given, than was done in the past, in the work and procedures of the General Staff at the Services Headquarters, as well as in the Command Headquarters and below, to long-term operational planning, including logistics as well as to the problems of co-ordination between various Services Headquarters. So, one major lesson learnt is that the quality of General Staff Work, and the depth of its prior planning in time, is going to be one of the most crucial factors in our future preparedness.

Direction of Operations

27. That brings me to the next point which is called the higher direction of operations. Even the largest and the best equipped of armies needs to be given proper policy guidance and major directives by the Government, whose instrument it is. These must bear a reasonable relation to the size of the army and state of its equipment from time to time. An increase

in the size or improving the equipment of the army costs not only money but also needs them.

Last Year's Reverses

28. The reverses that our Armed Forces admittedly suffered were due to a variety of causes and weakness as stated above. While this enquiry has gone deeply into those causes it has also confirmed that the attack was so sudden and in such remote and isolated sectors that the Indian Army as a whole was really not tested. In that period of less than two months last year, only about, 24,000 of our troops were actually involved in fighting. Of these, those in Ladakh did an excellent job even when overwhelmed and outnumbered. In the Eastern-most sector, though the troops had to withdraw in the face of vastly superior enemy strength from Walong, they withdrew in an orderly manner and took their toll. It was only in the Kameng sector that the Army suffered a series of reverses. These battles were fought on our remotest borders and were at heights not known to the Army and at places which geographically had all the disadvantages for our troops and many advantages for the enemy. But such initial reverses are a part of the tides of war and what matters most is who wins the last battle.

The Fourth Division

29. Before I end, I would like to add a word about the famous "Fourth Division", which took part in these operations. It is indeed said that this famous Division had to sacrifice its good name in these series of reverses. It is still sadder that this Division during the actual operations was only "Fourth Division" in name, for it was not fighting with its original formations intact. Troops from different formations had to be rushed to the borders to fight under the banner of the "Fourth Division", while the original formations of the Division itself were deployed elsewhere. I am confident, and I am sure the House would share with me that the famous "Fourth Division" would live to win many more battles if there is any future aggression against our country.

30. Before I conclude, I would like to mention that we have certainly not waited for this report to be in our hands to

take corrective action. The process of taking corrective action had started simultaneously with the institution of this enquiry and the House would recollect that I had informed it of the same.

31. What happened at a Se la and Bomdi La were severe reverses for us, but we must remember that other countries with powerful defence forces have sometimes suffered in the initial stages of a war. The aggressor of a certain advantage, more especially when the aggression is sudden and well-prepared. We are now on the alert and well on the way of preparedness, and this enquiry while bringing home to us our various weaknesses and mistakes would also help to strengthen our defence preparedness and our entire conduct of such operations.

Index